DEALING WITH STATUTES

JAMES S. CARPENTIER LECTURES

DEALING WITH STATUTES

JAMES WILLARD HURST

1982
Columbia University Press
New York

Clothbound editions of Columbia University Press books are Smyth-sewn and printed on permanent and durable acid-free paper.

Library of Congress Cataloging in Publication Data

Hurst, James Willard, 1910–
Dealing with statutes.

(James S. Carpentier lectures ; 1981)
Bibliography: p.
Includes index.
1. Statutes—United States. 2. Law—United States—Interpretation and construction. 3. Legislation—United States. I. Title. II. Series.
KF425.H87 349.73 81-10198
ISBN 0-231-05390-8 347.3 AACR2

Columbia University Press
New York Guildford, Surrey

Printed in the United States of America

JAMES S. CARPENTIER LECTURES

1904–5 JAMES BRYCE, VISCOUNT BRYCE
Law in Its Relation to History

1907–8 JOHN CHIPMAN GRAY
The Nature and Sources of the Law

1910–11 ARTHUR LIONEL SMITH
English Political Writers of the Seventeenth and Eighteenth Centuries and the Development of English Political Theory from Hobbes to Burke

DAVID JAYNE HILL
The Problem of World Organization as Affected by the Nature of the Modern State

1911–12 SIR FREDERICK POLLOCK
The Genius of the Common Law

1913–14 SIR COURTENAY ILBERT
The Mechanics of Law Making

1916–17 HAROLD DEXTER HAZELTINE
English Legal History

1919–20 WILLARD BARBOUR
English History with Special Reference to the Development of Rights through Procedure

1923–24 SIR PAUL VINOGRADOFF
Some Problems of Jurisprudence

1926–27 SIR WILLIAM SEARLE HOLDSWORTH
The Historians of Anglo-American Law

1927–28 BENJAMIN NATHAN CARDOZO
The Paradoxes of Legal Science

1940–41 SIR CECIL THOMAS CARR
Aspects of Administrative Law

1955 EDMUND MORRIS MORGAN
Some Problems of Proof under the Anglo-American System of Litigation

THOMAS REED POWELL
Vagaries and Varieties in Constitutional Interpretation

1956 GLANVILLE WILLIAMS
The Security of Life and the Criminal Law

1962 EDWIN W. PATTERSON
Law in a Scientific Age

1963 ELLIOTT EVANS CHEATHAM
A Lawyer When Needed

1965 LEON RADZINOWICZ
Ideology and Crime

1966 BENJAMIN KAPLAN
An Unhurried View of Copyright

1972 HENRY J. FRIENDLY
Federal Jurisdiction

1977 ARCHIBALD COX
Constitutional Adjudication under the Burger Court

1982 JAMES WILLARD HURST
Dealing with Statutes

CONTENTS

ACKNOWLEDGMENTS

I am grateful to the faculty of the School of Law of Columbia University for the invitation to deliver the James S. Carpentier Lectures from which these essays derive. My thanks go also to Dean Albert J. Rosenthal and his colleagues for providing a most hospitable forum for the lectures.

The essays develop themes which grow out of a long-term program of work in the social history of law in the United States. Over some years I have been indebted for support in this effort to the Social Science Research Council, the Rockefeller Foundation, the administration of the University of Wisconsin, and the trustees of the William F. Vilas Trust Estate, under whose auspices I hold a chair as Vilas Professor of Law at the University of Wisconsin. Of course the book does not purport to speak for any of these agencies; I take sole responsibility for what I have written.

James Willard Hurst

Madison, Wisconsin

DEALING WITH STATUTES

1

LEGISLATIVE PROCESS

Statute law is a pervasive element of twentieth-century legal order in the United States. More than constitutional law or common law, legislation and interpretation of legislation by lawyers, executive and administrative officers, and judges provide the bases for those parts of legal order which enter most broadly into people's everyday lives as well as into grand designs of public policy. Statute law directly embodies governing standards and rules for major sectors of life in society—for the market economy (as in the law of corporations and fair trade practices), for nonmarket factors (as in care for preserving the human stock and natural resources), for a general range of social institutions, (as in the law of associations or of the family). Statute law provides the legitimizing base and structure for the sweep of executive and administrative rules and orders which bulk so large in such fields as regulation of public utilities, corporate securities, marketing of food and drugs. Particularly in contrast stands the limited range of affairs determined by common law in the twentieth-century as compared with the prominence of common law in nineteenth-century public policy.

Yet the schools, the legal literature, and the legal profession have given remarkably little attention to the legislative process. Judge-made law is still the darling of the legal philosophers. Until recently legal historians have been content to piece together their stories almost wholly out of the action of courts.

In contrast these essays undertake to make the legislative product and its handling by lawyers, judges, and other public officers the focus of their concern. Courts figure largely in what I have to say, but for what they do with and within terms set by the statute books.

THE OPEN-DOOR JURISDICTION OF THE LEGISLATURE

Central to the practical importance of legislative process is the range of jurisdiction of legislatures over parties and subject matter. Early state constitutions set a pattern of conferring on legislatures the full extent of lawmaking authority originally confided to the Crown and Parliament together. From about the mid–nineteenth century on, states put into their constitutions some limits on legislative procedure and content, but typically these amounted to relatively narrow qualifications on what continued to be a broad endowment. The Federal Constitution enumerated the powers of Congress. But it did so for the most part in terms of standards rather than rules. Congressional practice and Supreme Court decisions developed the working content of these standards to authorize a range of national legislation comparable to the sweeping authority which the typical state constitution conferred on its legislature by simply vesting "the legislative power" of the state in that agency. Thus state and federal legislative jurisdiction opens the doors of the legislative branch more widely to petitioners than is the case with any other type of legal agency short of the process of constitutional amendment. The country's separation of powers tradition assigns an open-door policy to the legislative function. With only narrow exceptions any party may bring any subject into the legislative arena.[1]

This distinctive breadth of legislative jurisdiction stands out by contrast with the limits our tradition has set on approaching other agencies. However broad in total impact, executive or administrative lawmaking depends on statutory delegations which specialize the parties and subject matter with which such agencies may deal.[2] Lawmaking by judges is hedged in by doctrines of standing, justiciability, and precedent. But no formal barriers of standing limit access to a legislature. Anyone who can persuade a legislator to introduce a bill can cause the matter of his concern to be put into the legislative machinery.[3] Generally the legislature is free to make its own judgments of what matters are suitable for legislative consideration.[4] And the novelty of a proposal for legislation, or the fact that it will change prior common or statute law, raises no legal barrier to its adoption.[5] Not even constitutional limitations bar bringing the matter into the legislative arena. The legislators may vote down a proposal because they believe it to be unconstitutional. If the measure is adopted, a court may later hold it unconstitutional. But in the first instance the legislature may take it under consideration. To a point of order raised, whether a bill was properly before the chamber, the chair in the Wisconsin Assembly held "That there is no rule which says that unconstitutional bills shall not be considered."[6] And the Wisconsin Supreme Court refused to enjoin the secretary of state from publishing an act passed by the legislature: "We are here dealing with a bill which has not yet become a law [because not published according to the stipulations of the state constitution]. There is no such thing known to the law as an unconstitutional bill. A Court cannot deal with the question of constitutionality until a law has been duly enacted and some person has been deprived of his constitutional rights by its operation. . . . [N]o court has jurisdiction to enjoin the legislative process at any point."[7]

The open-door principle governing legislative jurisdiction gains emphasis from the fact that there are almost no judicially enforcible procedural limits on how the legislature does its business. Procedural due process does not require that legislators investigate relevant facts and values before they vote a statute; they are entitled to act on the basis of the knowledge they bring with them when they are elected.[8] Of course prudent promoters are likely to lay a foundation for a bill by hearings, against possible later issues in court over substantive constitutionality or interpretation. But they are under no constitutional procedural compulsion to do so.[9] There is no procedural due process requirement that the legislature give notice or opportunity to be heard to those who may be affected by proposed legislation. In practice legislatures today are likely to provide some notice and opportunity to appear in hearings. But they do so wholly at their discretion. [10] When legislative committees hold hearings, for most purposes they have the last word on their procedures, free of limits set for court proceedings by constitutions or by the law of evidence. Court-made rules of evidence do not govern; in particular, legislative hearings need not conform to rules against hearsay. The order of presenting evidence is wholly in the committee's discretion; whether affected parties have opportunity to attempt rebuttal or timely rebuttal of adverse material is up to the committee. Rarely do committees allow affected parties to cross-examine those who present hostile material; the committee alone decides whether there shall be any cross-examination.[11] There is some precedent for courts to apply to legislative hearings the privilege against self-incrimination and constitutional limits on search of papers, but this doctrine presents only narrow qualifications on the general discretion conceded to legislative process.[12]

Of course facts limit access to legislatures, though the law does not. Inequalities of means and of sophistication among affected interests limit those which make themselves effectively heard. This reality is reflected in the fact that weak interests have sometimes received some accounting, however inadequate, in actions in court, long before they have elicited legislative response.[13] The rise of the administrative process in large part responded to felt needs to provide support for interests which because of their diffuse character or lack of resources could not win direct action from legislators.[14]

Nonetheless, with all the limitations imposed by the realities of unequal means, knowledge, and skill of petitioners, the open-door character of legislative jurisdiction has given a distinctive place to legislative process. In the country's experience statute law has had special importance in giving content to public policy and adapting the legal-social order to changing currents of interest and circumstances.

THE UNIQUE ARRAY OF LEGISLATIVE POWERS

Legislatures in the United States possess an array of powers unique to them among legal agencies and unique in potential leverage on society. Throughout the country's life legislators have generally fallen far short of realizing their potential influence. That record of default and fumbling forms an important dimension of United States legal history. But the record cannot be explained by want of endowment; the endowment has always been rich. It has been so rich that even with disappointing performance the legislative branch has played distinctive and critical roles in shaping public policy.

In the light of both legislative practice and judicial doctrine, consider this endowment of legislative power as it has been in the second half of the twentieth century.

Defining Standards and Rules. U.S. legislatures possess the broadest authority of any agency short of the makers of a constitution to define standards and rules of official and private conduct in society. The chapter headings and indexes of twentieth-century federal and state statute books quickly reveal how far legislators have gone in preempting from common law the governance of most important areas of policy, ranging from such fields as market regulation to public utilities, to consumer protection, to public health and sanitation, to conservation of natural resources.[15] A long-standing example of the influence of statute law relative to judge made law is courts' reference to statutory standards or rules of conduct to determine whether a defendant's behavior should be deemed negligent so as to render him liable for damages for personal injury inflicted on another.[16] More recent examples of the felt impact of substantive statute law appear when courts imply legislative intent to provide civil remedies to implement statutory standards or rules beyond conventional areas of tort law. The United States Supreme Court cautions that provision of remedies depends on legislative intent, and that judges should require substantial demonstration of such intent.[17] Nonetheless, over the years the main current of decisions has been favorable to finding authorization of sanctions to promote substantive legislative policy, though the legislature has not explicitly provided them.[18]

Taxing, Borrowing, and Spending. Its powers to tax, borrow, and spend allow the legislature a role in allocating economic resources in substantial competition with the allocation role of the private market. The impress of this fiscal authority has been broad. In the public sphere it shows particularly on the spending side, for example, through creation of public services, through government contracting, and through government provision of high-risk capital in developing scientific knowledge and science-based, advanced technologies, as for ventures in space.[19] In the private sphere it shows in the by-products of such appropriation policies, and also powerfully in the ways in which twentieth-century tax law pervades entrepreneurial calculations and operates as forms of economic regulation by defining taxable income, setting terms of depreciation allowances, or providing investment tax credits.[20]

Creating New Forms of Organization. Legislatures have authority to create new forms of organization for public or private collective action. Constitutional tradition denies our executive officers the inheritance of Crown prerogative. Thus here the executive has no inherent power to charter private associations nor any general authority to set up official agencies.[21] At common law judges hold authority to name special masters or referees in aid of court functions, and are empowered to enforce private agreements for associated action or to declare agreements unenforcible or illegal as offending established public policies. But tradition holds such authority within narrow bounds; and in the field of non-official association the initiative of creation and implementation lies chiefly with private persons.[22] In contrast, legislators hold plenary power to create public executive or administrative agencies, specialized for particular fields of policy. They may create public-function corporations, such as the Tennessee Valley Authority. They may provide for chartering business corporations in all their variety of twentieth-century uses from small to giant enterprises. They may create nonprofit, philanthropic, and lobbying associations.[23] Finally, legislatures have authority to mandate or influence creation of procedures governing relations among public and private institutions and individuals. Thus Congress has created the envi-romental impact statement as a requirement of agency operations subject to the National Environmental Protection Act. So through broader federal statutory protection for consumers Congress has encouraged business corporations to revise their customer warranty policies.[24] Legislative power is thus deeply involved in the evolving institutional structure of the society, both public and private.

Investigating. The legislature has authority to investigate matters of fact and of fact-enmeshed values which it judges likely to be of public concern and relevant to possible legislation, and to do so substantially free of judicially enforcible limits on the subject matter it chooses to examine. In the later twentieth century the Supreme Court has cautiously offered some protection to unwilling witnesses where legislative inquiry, without a showing of strong overriding public interest, burdened freedom of speech or association.[25] The only constitutional limits the courts have enforced on the procedures for exercising this power are the privilege against self-incrimination and the ban on unreasonable search and seizure.[26] Judges have put some procedural limits on investigations where they could find that by statute or rule of their chambers legislators had set limits on the ways in which their committees conducted investigations.[27] In some respects the power of investigation has been the most important of the distinctive powers of the legislative branch. Potentially and to some measure in practice, the power has come to bear on all other legal agencies and on the general community over the widest range of social concerns. For the most part legislators have made such uneven and narrowly focused use of the power that they have fallen short of realizing its potential.[28] Nonetheless, within the limits of legislative practice, the use of the investigatory power has had substantial effects on various circles of affected interest. For lawyers, resort to this authority has provided another forum apart from courts or administrative agencies in which to represent clients. For inter-agency relations, the legislative authority to ask questions has provided the principal practical procedure for reviewing executive and administrative activity, especially when appropriations committees have examined budgets. For the general community the investigatory power has provided means of arousing or mobilizing public opinion, of educating people to identify their interests, and of providing bases for the legitimization of public policy programs. Early twentieth-century examples of the mingling of these functions and its impact on public policy can be seen in the Pujo Committee inquiry of 1911 into the practices of large banks, investment banking houses, and other financial intermediaries, which contributed to enactment of the Federal Reserve Act of 1913, and in the later investigations of banking and securities practices which dramatized the need for reforms that were embodied in the Glass-Steagall Banking Act of 1933.[29]

USE OF LEGISLATIVE POWERS AND THE LEGISLATIVE ROLE

Framers of the first state constitutions in this country, without definition or qualification, granted to elected assemblies what they simply termed "legislative power." They assumed that the grant had sufficient definition from precedents set by the conduct of Parliament, especially as Parliament had enlarged its fields of action since 1688 at the expense of older claims of Crown prerogative.[30] From the English Bill of Rights (1689) and from John Locke's Second Treatise of Civil Government they drew the principle that for a legal order capable of promoting a strong society while respecting individual rights the legislature should be first among the principal parts of government. It should be the prime source of general policy. Legislation should treat all individuals on equal terms and should care for the common interest. The legislature should be armed with exclusive control of the public purse, stand bulwarked against invasion by the executive and be committed not to delegate away its powers to other agencies.[31]

The sweep of authority thus readily granted to legislatures was understandable in the context of the times. The years of gathering tension with England had taught the colonists to rely on their elected representatives in the lower house of colonial legislatures as legal spokesmen for their interests. Legislative committees carried much of the burden of executive work in carrying on the Revolutionary War. From the conflict we developed deep suspicion of executive or administrative authority, which had been symbolized by royal governors and by the Board of Trade in London. To advance our interests we had not depended on lawsuits before colonial judges, who held office only at the pleasure of the Crown. Thus early state constitutions often denied the governor a veto or the possibility of patronage power through control of appointments, while in effect conferring wholly open-ended lawmaking power on the legislators.[32]

Legislative expansion of the money supply and provision of relief for distressed debtors in times of depression later led politically effective conservative forces to put some restraints on state legislative authority. This theme appeared in the framing of the Federal Constitution, notably in clauses forbidding the issue of bills of credit or enactment of laws impairing the obligation of contract. The Federal Constitution and later state constitutions took care to provide the chief executive with a veto power over legislation. From about the mid–nineteenth century, concern over rash ventures into public financing of transportation improvements led to the creation of state constitutional limitations on state debt and on state participation in works of internal improvement. Outpourings of special statutory franchises and corporate charters created fears that private interests were manipulating legislatures for selfish gain and perhaps by corrupt means, and in any case aroused objections to burdens on legislative dockets; in response, from the middle to the late nineteenth century lawmakers wrote into state constitutions procedural requirements that would promote more open policy making (stipulations as to reading bills and providing adequate titles) and bans on a wide range of special or local legislation. Yet these limitations amounted to relatively marginal subtractions from the broad potential of the core grant of "legislative power" under both early and later state constitutions.[33] The framers of the Federal Constitution did not make such a blanket grant to Congress, but enumerated the categories of its lawmaking authority. However, most of their provisions took the form of general standards rather than particularized rules. In the long run Congressional practice and interpretation by the Supreme Court read these standard clauses expansively, so that their total effect was to confer the functional equivalent of the broad authority given state legislatures.[34]

In the first three quarters of the nineteenth century the performance of Congress and the state legislatures showed relatively limited and unskillful use of their endowments. The bulk of the statute books consisted of highly particularized measures; statutes of broad policy or general reach were relatively few and reflected little bold programming or implementation. The state scene especially showed highly fragmented, ad hoc, unorganized lawmaking; for example, in Wisconsin between the first legislature of 1849 and the legislature of 1872 (following amendment of the constitution to forbid most special or local legislation), each year a pencil-thin volume of "general" laws stood dwarfed alongside a two- to four-inch-thick volume of "private and local" laws. The impression of fragmented, ad hoc, unorganized legislative action is not mistaken. This was for the most part the character of early and mid–nineteenth-century legislative process. Sessions were short. Most legislators were inexperienced in government, and there was substantial turnover in membership. Committee systems were undeveloped and committees had no staff to contribute continuity or learned skill. There was no sustained tradition of policy leadership from the White House. State constitutions had created a weak executive, and until the end of the nineteenth century state governors set no precedents for programming legislative action.[35]

Among the four areas of authority on which twentieth-century legislators have drawn to a large extent, two figured relatively little in the nineteenth century. In the logic of legislative operations the power of investigation might be expected to claim first place, in order to provide the necessary basis of facts and values for the making of public policy. It is not surprising that, with little experience or continuity and no staffing, nineteenth-century legislatures made little use of their investigatory power. Congress was more active, but typically it limited itself to investigating the conduct of the executive—the classic core of Parliamentary precedent for the investigating power. Not until the twentieth century does the record show broad-ranging Congressional inquiry into the market or other institutions or areas of conduct outside the operation of government agencies.[36]

So, also, nineteenth-century legislators made little use of their potential for setting standards or rules of behavior in the general community. At least for the years before the 1870's this outcome does not seem to have been the product of any doctrinaire philosophy of laissez faire. True, society committed to market dealings the regulation of the bulk of decisions on allocating economic assets. But through most of the century this pattern reflects more a taken for granted acceptance of the administrative utility of the market than the product of a felt need to protect the market from threat of legislative invasion; legal protection of market autonomy emerged more through common law than through legislative contests.

That common law figures so largely in the allocation of responsibility for social order between market processes and legal processes was part of a broader pattern prevailing until the end of the nineteenth century. Through these decades judge-made law provided the bulk of law governing trade in land, market transactions in goods and services, private investment, and security for loans, as well as law governing the allocation of loss in personal injury situations, definition of ordinary crimes, and determination of the incidents of domestic relations. The bursting growth of the society required law for a wide range of human concerns. But the nineteenth-century legislative process lacked the resources of tradition, experience, or operating skill to meet the demand. In contrast, litigation provided tradition, experience, and familiar operating skills, within which judges could define standards and rules of conduct for large areas of human relations. Contemporary society more readily accepted lawmaking by judges because people so often saw problems as calling for relatively limited adjustment of one-to-one confrontations—between buyer and seller, mortgagor and mortgagee, tortfeasor and victim, husband and wife. Legislation bulked larger in social regulation when more numerous and varied interests began to press claims for attention, and when politically effective opinion sensed a need to bring more factors into policy calculations. In that context both petitioners and lawmakers began to realize the process implications of the open-door jurisdiction of the legislative branch in contrast to the narrower avenues of access to judicial lawmaking.[37]

Despite its obvious imperfections and limitations, nineteenth-century legislative process was by no means without vitality in the two other principal domains of authority. From our national beginnings statute law embodied major components of social and legal order. Recognition of this fact may be useful as a caution against underestimating twentieth-century legislative process because of the imperfections we see in it.

Nineteenth-century legislation played major roles in resource allocation. Into the late nineteenth century the society was chronically short of fluid economic resources; it operated with a cash-scarce economy. In that setting the taxing and spending powers naturally did not have the prominent place they have held in the twentieth century. States made some direct investments in internal improvements in the second quarter of the nineteenth century, often with unfortunate results. Congress learned that it could raise substantial money by the tariff; sectional tensions showed that this approach also carried political risk, but it was administratively practicable.[38] Congress also affected economic allocations by measures to regulate the supply of money and credit, first under the two Banks of the United

States, then under the currency issues and national banking laws that originated in the North's financing of war. National regulation of the money supply was short-lived through the Banks of the United States, and inept thereafter, but still constituted major interventions in the economy.

The federal Constitution barred states from direct issues of money. But the Supreme Court ruled that the Constitution left states free to charter private commercial banks empowered to issue circulating notes. Until Congress imposed an effective prohibitive federal tax in 1865, such bank notes furnished much of the country's currency. In any case, credit—deposit-check money—provided by state-chartered and nationally chartered banks came to furnish the bulk of the money supply, again within policy frames set by statute law.[39] Functionally, though not in form, the disposition of public lands under terms set by legislation was a major use of the legislative power of the purse in the nineteenth century. Congress used the national public domain as a substitute for cash, using land to pay soldiers' bonuses, to subsidize creation of roads, canals, railroads, and educational facilities, and above all to furnish a low-cost capital base for developing a family farm economy in the Mississippi Valley, and indirectly for encouraging entry of private mortgage money to promote that economy. With lands granted them by Congress under statutory conditions, states were able to pursue similar policies on a more restricted scale.[40]

In the nineteenth century Congress and the state legislatures also made large-scale, vigorous use of their authority to create or legitimize new forms of public and private organization. Congress set up federal executive offices and bureaus dealing with an increasing range of programs. The state executive branch remained small and inconspicuous through most of the century, but state statutes by the hundreds provided the agencies and procedures of local government. Congress made limited use of the sources on which it might draw to create federally chartered corporations, except in the case of national banks. But in the face of much polemic against special privilege, from the 1830's on state legislatures chartered business corporations by the thousands, laying the foundations for the future role of the kind of organization that would dominate the private market and take on increasing social influence. Until the last quarter of the nineteenth century most provisions for local government and private corporations were by local and special statutes. This surge of particularized laws was an inefficient burden on legislative operations, created wasteful and often arbitrary differences where standardized treatment would have been sensible, fostered some abuses for special gain, and in any event bred damaging suspicion of abuse. Nonetheless, the total impact on public and private affairs was great and in large part constructive. Moreover, beneath surface differences, much of this special and local legislation carried major similarities of form and substance. Thus, as more and more standard provisions appeared in special corporate charters, the character of general corporation laws began to emerge from specially enacted statutes. The proper legislative business of generalizing public policy was underway amid the fragmented forms of the legislative product.[41]

Whatever the limitations of its role earlier, in the twentieth century the legislature has used its distinctive array of powers to make it the principal agency in legitimizing the premises and content of public policy. In the 1980's public policy had become most broadly defined and authenticated not in common law but in statute books. Moreover, its special armory of powers made the legislative branch an indispensable partner in the detailed policy making of executive and administrative offices and agencies. Some aspects of twentieth-century legal order raise questions about this estimate of the legislative role. But on reappraisal that role still appears to be central.[42]

Chief executives eventually emerged as leading sources of initiative of will to obtain passage of bills. Under Washington, Hamilton's reports on monetary and fiscal policy set early precedents for presidential leadership, not only in mustering the will to action but also in fashioning the substance of programs. Jefferson seized the opportunity to lead Congress in implementing the purchase of Louisiana. Jackson led the successful battle against renewing the charter of the second Bank of the United

States. Lincoln committed the North to resist secession. However, these were exceptional instances in the general course of the nineteenth century Presidency.[43] Not until Theodore Roosevelt do we encounter such sustained effort at directing lawmaking policy from the White House as people had come to accept and expect by the 1980's as a responsibility of presidential office.[44] In smaller measure and with less effect, the office of governor has also become in the twentieth century a source of energy for directing legislative effort.[45] Twentieth-century legislation empowering the President and state governors to frame and present executive budgets has provided the most continuing, detailed forms of executive guidance of legislative action.[46]

However, in major programs the role of the chief executive was apt to be not to lead in fashioning the content of policy, but rather at a critical juncture to supply energy of will and effective persuasion to move ahead policy proposals that originated and got their substance elsewhere. More often than not in the background of new policy stood a record of substantial activity in the legislative arena—of facts and ideas developed, alliances formed, bills introduced, drawn, and modified, hearings held and bargains struck among competing interests, while such activity before the legislature helped build supporting community opinion as a base for action. To note this is not to deny the importance of some executive interventions to press matters to decision. For example, initiatives of executive will were critical in 1935 when Franklin Roosevelt urged enactment of a social security system, and in 1964, 1965, and 1968 when Lyndon Johnson obtained passage of civil rights legislation.[47] But usually Presidents or governors could exercise effective leverage because a prior course of events in the legislative forum had prepared occasions for action. No other agency besides the legislature offered comparably broad access or facilities to explore new policy proposals or could provide the ultimate means of implementing existing programs. Nor did any other agency open so broad a field for maneuver of allied or competing interests, for trial and error testing of proposals for using law, and for bargaining out the development of general policy.[48]

In the twentieth century the growth of specialized executive offices and administrative agencies has provided the detailed content to fill out a wide range of statutory directives. Nineteenth-century judges declared flatly that legislators lacked authority to delegate power, but found formulas which in fact allowed an increasing amount of delegation. By the 1920's declared doctrine was that legislators might delegate rule-making power, if the authorizing statute laid down adequate standards to guide and confine the delegates.[49] Thereafter through the twentieth century in practice legislators sometimes set out guidelines in terms that were vague or highly uncertain in meaning. But courts showed themselves extremely reluctant to invalidate statutes for improper delegation; in effect they gave great weight to the presumption of constitutionality in this area.[50] Without pressing through to the constitutional issue, judges might exercise an intermediate level of review by finding that the administrators had exceeded the authority the legislature intended to give them; such a ruling could work as a remand to the legislature for a more precise redrafting of its mandate. However, courts did not show themselves markedly eager to wield even this qualified review.[51] In any event, however we rate the number of improper or loose delegations, the upshot by the 1980's was that the bulk of the detailed law in many important fields of regulation was contained not in statutes but in rules made by executive or administrative officers.

Granted the important contributions made by executive or administrative activity, the role of the legislature has continued to be of basic importance. Executive and administrative agencies owe their legal existence to statute law. Statutes define and create their jurisdiction over subject matter and persons. Statutes provide their funds and authorize the procedures they adopt.[52] Legislators make less use than they might of their investigatory powers. However, especially in Congress, legislative committees dealing with the subject matter of policy have established influential relations with relevant agencies in areas of sustained legal action.[53] And in any event the necessity of appropriations has brought recurring budget hearings through which legislative committees have examined particular uses of delegated authority and in effect have ratified or procured alterations in what their delegates were doing.[54] The roles of legislative committees are a reminder that legislation is in important measure a continuing process. An original delegation may be tentative and general, but may gain more legislative direction by amendments of the governing statute, or indeed by legislative silence in the face of administrative action or court rulings brought specifically to the attention of legislators.[55] Finally, we should note that in large part statutes have set the terms on which judges may review the procedures and substance of executive and administrative action; given the part of courts in developing the detailed content of policy, such statutory channeling of judicial review carries weight.[56]

In appraising the place of statute law in our twentieth-century legal order we need to take account of the fact that statutes do not execute themselves. Their practical impact is determined by the ways in which affected private persons or groups, lawyers in private practice and government lawyers, executive or administrative officers, and judges interpret them. Even if legislative draftsmen have been skillful and reasonably precise, and even if legislators have not shirked the responsibility of making reasonably clear choices of ends and means, the variety of circumstances and human behavior ensure that there will be room for interpretation to add content to what is in the statute books. Courts recognize this reality, for example, when they declare that they are not bound to apply legislation according to a rigidly literal reading of its language.[57] So also, when they give weight to contemporaneous, consistent, unchallenged, practical construction of any act "by the men charged with the responsibility of setting its machinery in motion, of making the parts work efficiently and smoothly while they are yet untried and new."[58] There is no need now to explore this aspect of affairs further; the second of these essays examines problems of statutory interpretation in some detail. Here it is relevant to note that the practical importance of discretion exercised in interpreting statutes does not negate the central place of statute law. Interpretation goes on within a context provided by legislative process. In the twentieth century the tendency has been for the elaboration of legislative records and the cumulative growth of statutory texts to add substantial content to that context.[59]

Apart from interpreting statutes, judges in our system may also modify the position of statute law by passing on the constitutionality of legislation. Under this authority between 1870 and 1930 courts asserted broad discretion to exercise their own judgment on the reasonableness of legislation regulating private activity in market. Thereafter the United States Supreme Court has led the way in substantially withdrawing judicial review of legislation dealing with public or private allocation of economic resources. But in the last half of the century the Court has also led in enlarging judicial review to implement Bill of Rights guarantees on behalf of groups disadvantaged by laws turning on racial, ethnic, or gender criteria, as well as on behalf of free political processes and values of free speech and press both in and apart from political process.[60] Both earlier and later styles of judicial intervention have inclined different sets of critics to conclude that judges were improperly preempting policy making. Again, there is no need now to pursue this matter in detail; the third of these essays explores the course of judicial review. Here it is appropriate, though, to put the exercise of judicial review in proper perspective relative to the overall position of statute law. Measured against the whole sweep of legislative activity, relatively little legislation has ever passed under judicial review, let alone been ruled invalid, in either the nineteenth or the twentieth century. Courts have not had to deal with constitutional challenges to the bulk of everyday affairs carried on under statutes laying taxes, providing public services (education, roads, health care, social security), setting frames of behavior of business corporations, or regulating markets to protect the wellbeing of workers, consumers, or the general public. On most matters most of the time, legislative practice and legislative judg-

There are some respects in which a focus on process rather than on outcome makes sense. In this society of such minute division of labor and such great diversity of interests, most people find that they are not actually interested in or materially affected by the particular substantive outcome of many questions brought to law. In morals and in economy—life energies are finite—it is proper that on many matters most of us decide that for us the public interest lies simply in the availability of a peaceful, reasonable process of decision.[68] We have also learned in our experience that there is a sensible mingling of concern with process and that with substance. The constitutional standard was that legislatures should act out of prime concern for the public interest and not merely for private interest. But legislative practice early established that the legislature should not refrain from doing what it reasonably believed would serve a public interest merely because its action might also concurrently bring special gain to some private interest. The Supreme Court has in effect accepted this principle. This approach makes moral and practical sense. In a society of rich variety of pursuits many statutes aiming at public interest goals are likely also to produce particularized gains and losses. The legislature could not serve the general welfare at all if it could act only where its action would produce no mingling of public and private gains.[69]

However, there are good reasons why we should not allow acceptance of the bargaining process to preempt attention to its substantive products. Two warnings from our past remain pertinent, though they point to different dangers. Tocqueville cautioned that in a society marked by formal legal equality coupled with a strong cultural bias toward exalting the economy and the creature comforts it could provide, there was danger that majority opinion would tyrannize over individuals. Broad popular sentiment can foster bargains struck in the legislative arena at the expense of fair regard for the worth and dignity of individuals or limited groups.[70] On the other hand, Calhoun warned that majorities may be artificial, opportunistic coalitions of particular interests temporarily joined to obtain their respective ends; legislative bargaining might well produce only seeming consensus

ment and not court orders have determined the uses of legislative authority.[61]

RELATION OF THE LEGISLATIVE BRANCH TO THE ORDER AND VITALITY OF THE SOCIETY

By virtue of its open-door jurisdiction, its distinctive array of powers, and its structure, the legislative branch has had special impact in determining the vitality of collective effort in this society, and the quality of social order. The record shows pluses and minuses; the elements that have shaped the character of legislatures have given them strength and have also in some respects made them weak or harmful to the general interest. But, however we strike the net balance between strength and weakness under one head or another of legislative activity, legislative process shows itself important in the course of public policy over more than two hundred years. Comprehensive assessment of legislative roles ranges beyond the scope of this essay. Consider, however, three salient areas of mixed promise and fulfillment, threat, and disappointment in legislative performance: the relation of the legislature to interest bargaining, to the need of leverage for action, and to the challenge of meshing generalization and particularization of public policy.

Bargaining. The legislature provides the broadest legal arena for peaceful, relatively rational and open negotiation among diverse interests. "The regulation of these various and interfering interests forms the principal task of modern legislation," Madison observed in *Federalist* No. 10.[62] The need for such a forum grew with the growth of the society. Calhoun in effect prophesied so in 1830 when he cautioned that "the more extensive and populous the country, the more diversified the condition and pursuits of its population, and the richer, more luxurious and dissimilar the people, the more difficult it is to equalize the action of the government and the more easy for one portion of the community to pervert its powers to oppress and plunder the other."[63]

The structure of the legislative branch invited a prime role in legal adjustment of interests. The expansive grants of "legislative power" in the states and the broad standards set for Congressional subject matter authority in the Federal Constitution opened doors wide to petitioners and to proposals old or new, conventional or novel. Legislative chambers stood on broad electoral bases. Distinctions between lower and upper houses in size of constituency and length of term fostered different alignments of bargainers. Limited tenure related to limited constituency areas kept legislators sensitive to distribution and intensity of interests among voters. The absence of formal external controls on legislative investigation and hearings gave legislators practical scope for exploring, testing, and maneuvering among interests. The strong potential in the legislature's distinctive array of powers made that branch a magnet attracting outsiders to seek services, subsidies, legitimization, or regulation. In comparison the course of common law proceeded within relatively narrow constraints of tradition, precedent, and sharply focused controversies, and executive or administrative lawmaking—however dense and weighty in specialized detail—depended on legislative assignment of jurisdiction and supplies.[64]

The facilities the legislature offers for fashioning public policy out of bargaining among interests raise difficult value issues which will never find final resolution. Bargaining through legislative process has positive worth for fairness and restraint against abuse of power, as against monopoly of policy by executive power or by the zeal of one-issue lobbies. But experience shows that such bargaining carries some risks and costs that are difficult to deal with.

There is danger of stalemate in the face of situations which call for positive response to deal with relations that are out of joint. In the twentieth century the rise of bureaucratized lobbies capable of raising substantial funds has increased the tendency toward stalemate; these groups cannot always obtain a positive response from legislators, but can exercise strong practical vetoes on lawmaking. In the last half of the twentieth century legislators' dependence on the political parties has tended to

decline, weakening party leadership. Sometimes t
ecutive has supplied impetus to action, but usua
executive intervention has depended on a good d
already done in the legislative forum. Courts' deci
interpretation or constitutionality of statutes have
spurred legislative response, but this factor has op
radically, subject to the varied chances and hazards of

Though legally the legislative doors stand wide
qualities in knowledge or operating skills or in mo
unequal access to the bargaining arena. This is a prol
as our legislatures; consider Shays' Rebellion in Mas
in 1786, or in 1790-91 the frustrated anger of his op
the superior discipline and sophistication Hamilton
for the fiscal and monetary policies he steered thro
gress.[66] Lawmakers sought to meet this problem wi
restructurings of process, notably by regulating use
in politics and in lobbying, and by creating administra
cies to provide specialized skill, experience, and will
behalf not only of interests weak for lack of wealth b
those weak primarily because they were diffuse. By int
in legislative proceedings or by the veto, chief executiv
times acted for broader constituencies than those fo
lobbies spoke. By enforcing standards of legally fair r
tation in legislatures against malapportionment or ge
ders, federal and state courts had some influence for mo
access to legislative bargaining processes. Such factors c
the problem of inequality. At base, however, it was th
and diversity of interests that managed to wield influen
bargaining arena which made the legislative branch o
importance in containing social tensions and legitimatin
policy.[67]

Another danger in relying on interest group bargai
fashion policy is that the process tends to become an
itself. Lawmakers and constituents may grow too ready to
that the public interest lies simply in having a workab
gaining process, rather than in producing desirable subst
results.

at the cost of more real public interest.[71] In the Cold War fears of the 1950s repressive use of legislative investigatory power and of executive regulation of public and some private employment under statutory delegation showed the contemporary relevance of Tocqueville's concern.[72] In the second half of the twentieth century Calhoun's artificial majorities have flourished and grown deep roots of vested interest, as lobbies, legislative committees, and regulatory agencies built their own tight circles of mutual profit and protection.[73] The legislature's principal resource against such fragmentation of policy has been its capacity to create broad new premises of public action, as it has done in creating a framework for labor-management peace, or for social security.[74] As Tocqueville predicted, by enforcing the Bill of Rights either in constitutional rulings or by interpreting statutes to favor Bill of Rights values, courts have put some check on legislative submission to popular fear and feeling.[75] Over-all, the record has been chequered enough to warn that we are naive if we trust legislative bargaining as a sure process for arriving at the public interest.

Leverage. The legislative process is cumbersome. Among competing interests some seek action, some want delay, some press for declaring general goals, some for pursuing special interest. Legislative committees and subcomittees are jealous of their subject-matter jurisdiction. Rules of the chambers may expedite business but may also provide ample opportunity for skilled parliamentary tacticians to maneuver or to stall action. Always in the background is competition for limited time. Sponsors must invest much effort simply in trying to get their proposals on the active agenda. More measures lose out in this competition for time than as the result of conflicts over substance. These factors together with the overriding preoccupation of legislators with getting elected or reelected operate to foster narrow pragmatism rather than concern for grand design as the normal temper of legislative bodies; prime energy typically focuses on what can be done here and now in particular detail.[76] Thus only at exceptional intervals of concentrated action has legislation provided major change, establishing broad new premises of policy. Outstanding examples are the years from about 1905 to 1915, in which both federal and state statutes launched the modern administrative process, the New Deal years, with their focus on new definitions of law's relations to market processes, and the mid-1960s with their emphasis on civil rights legislation. The intervention of chief executives to muster will to action figured in such bursts of high policy making. But legislative bargaining fixed the substance of what was done and it was statute law which legitimated the new goals and provided the authority for executive, administrative, and judicial officers to implement those goals.[77]

After due account of how legislatures usually behave, realism also calls for comparing the legislative process with the ways in which change proceeds in the general society and with the year in, year out conduct of other legal agencies. Such comparisons suggest that, despite its cumbersome and somewhat irregular energies, legislative process has been outstanding among our devices for affecting events. The unplanned impacts of mass use of the automobile—urban sprawl, costs in death and injury, heightened competition of highway funds with other public interest investment, air pollution—remind us how much of social experience is shaped by social inertia, and by our characteristic preoccupation with the most readily available ends and means in deciding what we will do. In analogous fashion most of the everyday activity of executive or administrative agencies or courts centers on the most immediately felt problems of choice or direction or with detailed implementation of goals already set. Of course it is sensible that neither private persons nor public officers should be constantly reexamining basic ends or procedures; great investment of time and energy is needed to make effective the goals we have already chosen. Moreover, given the limits of people's stocks of energy, will, and knowledge it would be unrealistic not to expect that a great deal of what comes about in society will always come about as the product of unplanned drift and cumulation of events. Granted these realities, the quality of life in society depends on increasing the extent of control we have over our experience.

In this country's lifetime the two principal institutions for enlarging control have been organized scientific and technological inquiry and legal processes. In the twentieth century among legal processes legislation has embodied the community's principal leverage for developing the major premises of public policy in taxation, education, transportation, care for the safety and health of workers and consumers, conservation of natural resources, regulation of the money supply and the integrity of financial institutions, promotion of peaceful labor relations, and provision of social security. Contributions of executive and administrative practice and of judicial administration have had no comparable place in framing most of twentieth-century institutional structure. That this has been so derives from the breadth of representative base and access marking the legislative branch, and from its distinctive array of powers. The leverage that legislative process affords for moving against social inertia and against the tendency of everyday private and public administration to center on narrow immediacies is critically important for social order. Here is a legal agency specially structured and empowered to deal broadly and in a sustained way with changing circumstances. In a constructive sense the legislative branch thus is a conservative agency; the likelihood of radically destructive social change increases in proportion as government is not responsive to changed circumstance, stands only for familiar vested interest, or is subject to the tyranny of small decisions or to the comfortable constraints of unquestioned custom and habit.[78]

Generalizing and Particularizing Policy. People and circumstances made demands on the law that sometimes called for establishing broad new principles of public policy (as in the 1930s commitment to use national fiscal and monetary powers to counter the depression), and sometimes for making highly specific decisions (as in the particular items of appropriations bills).

Effective response to demands to pursue new general goals typically required further specifying means to implement the goals (as in providing criteria and machinery for operating a system of unemployment compensation). The distinctive character of legal agencies derived considerably from the qualities and defects they showed in responding to needs for generalized and particularized policy.

In the nineteenth century the growth of common (judge-made) law was prominent in producing an effective mix of general and particular policy. With skill and insight, perceptive judges such as Chief Justice Shaw in Massachusetts developed general principles—for example, legal favor for free private association—that fit the working needs of the times. Concurrently the variety and concrete detail presented in lawsuits kept judges' policy close to earthy reality and allowed courts to test doctrine in action—advancing, qualifying, or retreating as particular experience might suggest.[79] However, common law policy making was inherently limited. It depended on the initiative and means of individual litigants, and on the issues presented by records made in specific suits. Accidents of the timing and scope of matters litigated might not bring to court matters of general concern when those matters needed attention or in circumstances fairly representative of the underlying problems. Judges had no independent means of investigating facts relevant to the policy choices involved, and they held a quite limited armory of means for dealing with affairs—chiefly judgments for money damages or decrees of injunction.[80]

Legislatures were better equiped than courts to reconcile the different demands of lawmaking processes entailed in making general determinations of policy on the one hand and particular determinations on the other. Untrammelled by formal limits on the standing of petitioners or on the subjects with which they might deal, they were broadly empowered to set new goals and contrive new procedures; commanding the public purse, they could invoke the flexibility of money resources to carry out programs; authorized to create new forms of organization, they could delegate to special agents the detailed pursuit of statutory purposes; armed with sweeping power to ask questions, they could inquire how executive or administrative officers spent the money the legislature allotted them, and how well or ill administrators' rules and orders served the ends set out in the governing statutes.

Twentieth-century legislators have used their equipment to bring into being and legitimate an expansive, often sprawling mix of general and particular law. Between 1810 and 1890 courts had created a great body of judge-made law. Between the founding decade of the modern administrative process, 1905–1915, and the 1980s, legislators and the executive and administrative officers in central and in local government to whom they delegated power produced a body of service and regulatory law that dwarfed the common law performance. Three types of situations were central to this development and lent themselves to responses that were consistent with traditional values embodied in the separation of powers. First, delegation was necessary where public interest goals required informed drafts on ordered, professional knowledge, as in regulating medicines or the use of nuclear energy. Second, delegation was necessary when the legislature decided that public interest required that the law intervene in complex affairs where no ordered body of knowledge or skill already existed to guide the regulators, and where protection of diffuse interests called for creating specialized centers of active will to enforce policy. Such felt needs produced administrative regulation of public utilities and of the issue of corporate securities and trading on stock exchanges. Third, delegation was necessary where implementing new public policy programs, such as a social security system, required promulgating large bodies of detailed and technical rules and creating procedures to handle a massive bulk of claims True, delegated legislation proliferated beyond the proper range of these three types of situations to an extent that did not always carry the same conviction of need. For better or worse, the sum of all this was a massive accomplishment, a prime fact of twentieth-century legal order.[81]

In the full surge of this development in the second half of the twentieth century legislators have fallen a good deal short of the degree of supervision of executive and administrative law making required by the principle of legislative supremacy. The responsibility here clearly lies with the legislature. In practice in this area judges have applied the presumption of constitutionality with such strength that decisions invalidating delegations have been rare. Challenge might be made in court that particular administrative rules violated substantive or procedural requirements of the governing statute. But, wary of the limits of their competence in matters calling for specialized knowledge or experience, judges have focused mainly on regularity of procedures, and have shown themselves reluctant to probe the substance of policy adopted by agencies to which the legislature has delegated broad authority.[82] Within the broad scope allowed them, legislatures have too often delegated power in vague or ambiguous terms. Appropriations hearings have provided some detailed scrutiny of the particularized law made by the legislature's delegates. But, despite large increases in staffing, legislative committees charged with substantive policy areas have made only irregular and limited use of their broad powers of investigation. Legislatures have betrayed uneasy conscience over the scope of discretion they have allowed their delegates by moving to grant to legislative committees certain powers of review of executive and administrative rules. This movement indicates the existence of tensions over recent working experience with the separation of powers. But this particular change was of dubious merit. It did not assure sustained, informed oversight by the relevant subject matter committees. It carried the danger of transferring to a committee forum the pressures of special interests which in that narrower arena might wield greater influence than they could before the legislature itself. The problems involved call for broader response than legislators have yet made.[83]

The need to effect a proper balance between responsibilities to make general policy, to respond by proper delegation to needs for more particularized development of policy, and to exercise effective supervision of executive and administrative agencies, has posed constant challenges to twentieth-century legislators. The nature of the demands people have been making on government since the turn of the century, and which experience teaches they will continue to make, indicates that the problems of relating general and particular policy are fixed firmly in the structure of the legal and social order. These problems will not go away. They present the principal challenge of the times to the conscience, skill, and experience of legislative lawmakers.

2

THE INTERPRETATION OF STATUTES

Interpreting a statute is likely to involve a good deal more than reading a printed text and measuring particular facts against the formula set by the words. Beyond the statute book may lie a potential clash of wills, affecting how far legislators effectively fix public policy and how far those who undertake to use the legislative product determine the working content of policy. In his 1908 Carpentier lectures John Chipman Gray observed that:

> It has been sometimes said that the Law is composed of two parts, legislative law and judge-made law but, in truth, all the Law is judge-made law. The shape in which a statute is imposed on the community as a guide for conduct is that statute as interpreted by the courts. The courts put life into the dead words of the statute.[1]

His statement underestimates the effects of legislative action, given the character of the legislature's powers, the capacities of statutory language, and the additional vitality that legislative history can sometimes contribute to statutory texts. Reflecting a deep-seated bias of writings on jurisprudence, Gray exaggerates the role of judges. Few of the multitude of choices people make everyday affected by what they find in statute books ever come before a court; what judges do is important, but it is outreached by the vast number of occasions on which laymen, lawyers, and executive and administrative officers make final decisions on the meaning of legislation. However, although he overstates, Gray points to a core reality. Statutory texts are rarely self-executing, but derive much of their impact from the uses others than legislators make of them.[2] It is regularly in order to ask, who is really in charge?

Various factors that normally operate in the legislative process tend to raise questions over who controls policy. Back of a statute of much consequence usually are competing or diverse interests which may produce bargains or adjustments in language often not fully spelled out, or deliberately left in some measure of uncertainty. After a statute is on the books, variety in situations and changes in circumstances pose questions to which the best drawn text will not always provide self-evident answers.[3] Thus we should be sensitive to the likelihood that in applying statute law separation of powers issues may be at stake. In particular cases, tension may exist among legal agencies over the relative degree to which legislators, administrators, or judges determine the practical content of policy formally declared in the statute books. It may exist between the public and private sectors, as official policy bears on positions pressed by suitors, by lawyers for clients, and by organized interest groups.

"THE INTENTION OF THE LEGISLATURE"

The standard criterion for proper interpretation of a statute is to find "the intention of the legislature." In 1930 Max Radin denied the validity of this formula in a challenge which has become a modern classic. He argued that the canon pursued a fiction; a legislative body in fact had no common intent, and could have none. Alternatively, he contended that if search revealed an actual legislative intent, that intent carried no legal title to govern application of the statute. Radin pursued his argument in extreme terms. But the uncompromising character of his analysis makes it a useful instrument to bring into focus basic matters of fact and questions of principle in dealing with statutes.[4]

To Radin the idea that in voting a particular text into the

statute book the legislature had a "series of pictures in mind," one of which was the particular situation now in issue, was a "transparent and absurd fiction."

> It is clearly enough an illegitimate transference to law of concepts proper enough in literature and theology. The least reflection makes clear that the law maker, *der Gesetzgeber, le legislateur*, does not exist, and only worse confusion follows when in his place there are substituted the members of the legislature as a body. A legislature certainly has no intention whatever in connection with words which some two or three men drafted, which a considerable number rejected, and in regard to which many of the approving majority might have had, and often demonstrably did have, different ideas and beliefs.[5]

Of course we use a fiction if we speak of the legislature as if it were a being of one mind. But so durable a fiction endures because it has a use validated by experience. This formula reminds all who deal with a statute that they are operating in a field of law in which they are not free to define public policy simply according to their own judgment.[6]

In this aspect the formula serves a function analogous to that of the charge to the jury in a suit to recover damages for injury alleged due to the defendant's negligence. We understand that when the judge tells the jurors to measure the defendant's conduct by the test of a reasonable and prudent individual, he is not referring them to the behavior of an identifiable, standardized creature housed in the state capitol like the official yard bar kept in the Bureau of Standards. He is reminding them that they sit as representatives of the community. As such they are not to judge the defendant by their wholly individual ideas of proper conduct, but are to try to step outside their own unique experience and feelings and apply criteria that reflect general experience and generally held values.[7]

In this light reference to legislative intention, insofar as it invokes a legal fiction, nonetheless serves useful functions for a lawyer. In his role as counsellor of a client, the formula admonishes him that he will not serve the client well if he disdains such objective limits of the law as the statute may indicate. As an advocate, he can invoke the formula to curb the will of the administrator or judge who seems inclined to give rein to his own preferences at the client's expense in disregard of statutory guidelines. As negotiator for his client he can draw on the formula to check the policy pretensions of his opposite number on the other side of the bargaining table. To public officers the formula stands as a ready reminder of their obligations under the separation of powers: that, as Heydon's Case declared (1584), having sought to learn "what remedy the Parliament hath resolved and appointed to cure the disease of the commonwealth" and what be "the true reason of the remedy", then "the office of all the judges is always to make such construction [as] . . . to add force and life to the cure and remedy, according to the true intent of the makers of the Act, *pro bono publico*."[8]

Radin presents two solid objections to the reality of a discoverable legislative intention.[9] First, that a statutory text of any substantial generality will normally prove capable of embracing too many and too diverse situations to allow lawmakers to foresee them all. Second, that legislators are too numerous and bring too many different perceptions and desires to their task to allow them to come to shared choices.

> The chances that of several hundred men each will have exactly the same determinate situations in mind as possible reductions of a given determinable, are infinitesimally small. The chance is still smaller that a given determinate, the litigated issue, will not only be within the minds of all these men but will be certain to be selected by all of them as the present limit to which the determinable should be narrowed.[10]

To appraise Radin's two points in light of typical patterns of legislative behavior helps us to locate points of effective power in the legislative process.

Radin puts his many-situations objection in a way that in large measure begs the question. The question posed by the search for legislative intent he says is, "Did the legislator in establishing this determinable [the general proposition set out in the statutory text] have a series of pictures in mind, one of which was this particular determinate [the specific situation to which someone proposes to apply the statute]?"[11] In effect he asks us to accept that legislative intent could have reality only in a fashion analogous to a reel of motion picture film—a succession of little frames, each freezing the image of a specific, focused condition of facts. In his statement of the problem, legislative intent can exist relevant to the particular occasion for which someone would invoke the statute only if that occasion has its specific counterpart in one of the frames of the reel of pictures the legislators ran through their minds as they decided whether to pass the bill before them. But this approach defines away the problem, rather than coming to grips with it.

Of course due to variety and change in human affairs it will often be true that the legislators did not forecast the particular condition or set of facts to which someone now suggests applying the statute. But they may well supply sufficient specifications to provide a discernible frame of reference within which the situation now presented quite clearly fits, even though it represents in some degree a new condition of affairs unknown to the lawmakers. An 1853 Massachusetts statute made it a felony knowingly to possess "an engine, machine, tool or implement adapted and designed for cutting through, forcing or breaking open a building, room, vault, safe or other depository, in order to steal therefrom money or other property." In 1940 the Massachusetts Supreme Judicial Court held that the statute applied to a defendant charged under this provision with possessing with the defined unlawful intent keys to the trunk locks of automobiles belonging to salesmen who were accustomed to carry goods in their cars and leave them there while they called on customers. The ruling seems to fit the manifest intent of the act, which was to penalize possessing an instrument which would give access without the owner's consent to a locked place of safekeeping of goods for the purpose of stealing the goods. The specific pictures actually drawn by the statutory text were here sufficient to cover the new type of situation that the course of events had produced.[12]

There is another range within which legislators can hold and adopt common purposes. There is a type of policy choice that looms large in the law, but that Radin blandly ignores when he asks us to accept his "series of pictures" as the only sense in which legislators could share intentions. Lawmakers can join in declaring general goals they want legal agencies to pursue, or a general range of means they want agencies to employ. The Sherman Act provides a stellar example. Its sweeping ban on "every contract, combination in the form of trust or otherwise, or conspiracy in restraint of trade or commerce among the several states or with foreign nations" perhaps goes to the verge of being unconstitutional for vagueness. Its legislative history adds little specificity to its definition, and its generality amounts to delegating broad authority to judges to spell out the particular content of its policy.[13] However, the Act manifested a real intent that the federal government assume some positive responsibility to check self-destructive tendencies in interstate markets, and to act to keep competition alive. Upholding the constitutionality of the Act, the Supreme Court spoke both for the reality and the legitimacy of generalization of public policy as an important part of the legislative function:

> So far as the arguments proceed upon the conception that in view of the generality of the statute it is not susceptible of being enforced by the courts because it can not be carried out without a judicial exertion of legislative power, they are clearly unsound. The statute certainly generically enumerates the character of acts which it prohibits and the wrong which it was intended to prevent. The propositions therefore but insist that, consistently with the fundamental principles of due process of law, it never can be left to the judiciary to decide whether in a given case particular acts come within a generic statutory provision. But to reduce the propositions, however, to this their final meaning makes it clear that in substance they deny the existence of essential legislative authority and challenge the right of the judiciary to perform duties which that department of the government has exerted from the beginning.[14]

Thus, dealing with a major interstate industry of the time of the Act's passage, the Court properly found within the indicated intent of Congress condemnation of a rate agreement among competing interstate railroads. Likewise, the indicated general intent of Congress was properly held to forbid otherwise proscribed conduct engaged in by an industry—the production of motion pictures—not in existence or foreseen when the Act was passed.[15]

Radin's second major objection to the possible existence of shared legislative intent is that there are many legislators, who must be expected to foresee different particular situations that might arise within a statutory formula, and to make different choices as to which situations would be included. This objection ignores the core reality of the division of labor in producing legislation. A statute is normally the product of the focused effort and detailed attention of a relatively few individuals involved in the legislative process—of sponsors, members of the relevant legislative committees, and the staff of the sponsors or committees. The committee is the key workplace of the legislature, as is recognized in the primacy judges give to committee reports as admissible evidence of legislative intent. If statutory text, with or without supporting legislative history, is capable of conveying a persuasive message from those thus specially involved, realism does not require looking further to find that a legislative intent exists and is known. To take this course does not ignore the general membership of the legislature. Again, if doctrine is to fit reality—and Radin advances his analysis as a contribution to a realistic jurisprudence—we should note that normally the role of the general membership is a cautionary, residual one, to promote responsible work by the specialists. Sponsors, committee members, and supporting staff have to do their particular work with the knowledge that at some point their product must pass the test of a vote by the whole body. Though only a few members may in fact vote on many bills, the process stands open for critics to rally a larger turnout; thus the limited circle that works up the bill must make such choices and adjustments as they calculate will pass muster before the larger body or not unduly arouse opposition there.[16]

In both of the principal objections to the reality of legislative intent Radin's analysis lacks realism in proportion as he implicitly treats each enactment as an isolated episode. In fact statute books show important lines of continuity and development of public policy. The effect of successive attention to like problem areas and of cumulative effort of successive groups of legislative specialists is often to sharpen the focus and build the detailed content of lines of statute law. Thus in 1929 the Supreme Court found ample basis for restrictively construing permission given in the immigration act to aliens to enter the country "temporarily for business:" "The various acts of Congress since 1916 evince a progressive policy of restricting immigration. The history of this legislation points clearly to the conclusion that one of its great purposes was to protect American labor against the influx of foreign labor."[17]

Beyond his argument against the reality of legislative intent, Radin seeks to persuade us that if there is such a thing as a discoverable intent of the legislature, it has no legal claim to be binding. This conclusion he derives from the "specialized function" of legislators:

> That function is not to impose their will even within limits on their fellow-citizens, but to 'pass statutes', which is a fairly precise operation. That is, they make statements in general terms of undesirable and desirable situations, from which flow certain results. As a rule, the statements must be made in the words of a specified language. A statute made in Latin at the present time is no statute, although the intention of the legislature can be as well or as ill made out from Latin as from English. . . . When the legislature has uttered the words of a statute, it is *functus officio*, not because of the Montesquieuan separation of powers, but because that is what legislating means. The legislature might also be a court and an executive, but it can never be all three things simultaneously.[18]

Much of this argument seems either legally wrong or beside the point. Of course people do not elect legislators "to impose their will" in any individualistic or arbitrary sense. But they do elect legislators to make choices designed to promote what legislators can reasonably deem to be the public interest. Some of these choices may be general, as in the Sherman Act; some may be quite specific, as in the line items of appropriations bills. In either instance they are choices given the force of law because they are made by a special body delegated to do so by a legally legitimated process of selection. Both to supervise the legislators and to adapt everyday behavior to the frame of public policy thus provided, people need to know what their delegates intend by the choices they have voted into the statute books.[19] That to be legally operative a statute must meet some requirements of form in no way detracts from the legal importance of determining its intended substance; at most, Radin's Latin reference reminds us that a statute may so far fail to communicate as to offend the standard of due process of law because it is so vague or unintelligible.[20] Certainly, that a statute must meet some requirements of form does not negate the relevance of its content. One can carry home a quart of milk only if it is in a container. This does not mean that the customer therefore has only a container and no milk. Moreover, in seeking to be guided by the legislature's intent we do not turn that body into a court or an executive. We simply respect its assigned function of providing authoritative guidelines to judicial and executive officers.[21]

The basic difficulty with Radin's argument is that he treats a statute as though it were a value-neutral tool to be used by lawyers, administrators, or judges for particular ends of their choosing, within the ample room he finds usually allowed by the minimum and maximum extension of statutory texts. He apparently would approve of the use of statutes much as a carpenter uses a saw or a hammer, choosing the instrument most efficient to what the user wants to accomplish. This attitude surfaces when he observes that the "purpose" of a statute need not be identified with "the actual purpose entertained by those who framed it or voted it"; in that sense "purpose" is the same as "intention", presenting the same difficulties that "this purpose is practically undiscoverable and would be irrelevant if discovered."

> But the purpose of many entities may be something far simpler and more apparent, something which is evident in the character of the thing itself, the end or final cause in the Aristotelian sense as distinguished from its efficient or its material cause. So, a razor

> is something to shave with, and we should know this without the least speculation as to the ideas which were in the manufacturer's mind when the razor was made.[22]

But a statute is not a "thing," a tool carrying in itself no obligation on the user in choosing the product for which he uses it. One may use a razor to sharpen pencils or to cut thread, rather than to shave, without thereby violating any obligation to the manufacturer. Using it to sharpen pencils may be inefficient by an economist's calculus of relations of inputs and outputs. But the use does not disobey a duty or infringe a function that society has authorized the manufacturer to impose on his customers. In contrast, a statute embodies a choice of values carrying obligations on those within its governance, backed by the force of the state. Under our constitutional arrangement of official powers, legislators may legitimately thus set guiding or limiting frames of action for other people. Because the statute's function is to make authoritative value determinations, fulfillment of the function is impossible without inquiry as to what values and what order of values the legislators had in mind. Inevitably those who put statutes to use must exercise considerable discretionary judgment on specifics that the legislators have not directly resolved. Also, they must exercise cautious wisdom in consulting materials outside the statutory text. But in the end the presence of the statute tells them that they deal with an area of public policy where not their value choices but those of a distinct body are to set the course. Radin's razor analogy points toward a range of free choice of values which our separation of powers tradition does not warrant for those who put legislation into operation.[23]

LEGISLATION AS PRODUCT OF A CONTINUING PROCESS

Next to the importance of acknowledging the criterion of legislative intent is the need to recognize that if legislation becomes a living part of social experience typically it does so as the result of a continuing process, only part of which is represented by putting words into a statute book. The roots of a process view of legislation run deep in our tradition. Though it derives from a quite different legal context than that within which we work, yet the general approach taken in *Heydon's* case (1584) is still timely, as the barons of the Exchequer there instruct us that

> for the sure and true interpretation of all statutes in general (be they penal or beneficial, restrictive or enlarging of the common law) four things are to be discerned and considered:
> 1st. What was the common law before the making of the Act?
> 2nd. What was the mischief and defect for which the common law did not provide?
> 3rd. What remedy the Parliament hath resolved and appointed to cure the disease of the commonwealth? And
> 4th. The true reason of the remedy, and then the office of all the judges is always to make such construction as shall suppress the mischief, and advance the remedy, and to suppress subtle inventions and evasions for continuance of the mischief, and *pro privato commodo*, and to add force and life to the cure and remedy, according to the true intent of the makers of the Act, *pro bono publico*.[24]

Note that *Heydon's* case in effect is saying that as a vital element in the community's life a statute is more than the text we find in the statute book. That text derives its vitality in part from its past—from the prior state of the law and the shortcomings of that state of law. The text derives its vitality in part from its future—from what those charged with applying it do to give it force, not only to promote its objectives but to overcome contrivances to evade its mandates. The statutory text is central and commands deference. But to grasp the full reality of its impact we should see it as part of a flow of policy-making activity.[25]

Twentieth-century courts in this country show themselves sensitive to legislation as typically the product of a continuing process. In contrast, nineteenth-century decisions were likely to treat a statute as an isolated item, though statute law was always a substantial element of the legal order. From about 1820 to 1890 the growth of common law captured the ambition and imagination of judges and legal writers to the extent that they tended to identify this sector as the true law compared with which legislation was marginal, exceptional, and indeed intrusive. They often expressed this attitude in unsympathetic reading of statutes, especially by invoking canons of construction which by their vagueness and diversity enlarged the judges' own freedom of choosing policy. But by the early twentieth century statute law had increased in reach and density to become the central element of law, showing sustained lines of policy as sturdy as judicial precedent. Legislators had become more knowledgeable, lobbies more organized, and legislative staffing, hearings, and committee work more systematized. This development, woven together with growth of delegated legislation, created a frame of reference for public policy far different from that of the nineteenth century.[26]

Judicial doctrine and techniques of dealing with legislation responded to these changes in four ways which, taken together, show a markedly different temper from that of the nineteenth-century decisions. The twentieth-century approach is to be prepared and willing to give weight to particular legislative history, to the pattern of succession of statutes in a given field, to the bearing of general sectors of legislation on particular acts, and to the course of practical construction of legislation by officials charged with putting it in operation.

Most influential are the reports of the legislative committees that considered the bill that became the statute. It is an appropriate emphasis, because the committee is normally the workplace in which members have hammered out the particular content of the measure.[27] Probably next in consequence are inferences to be drawn from comparing the original text of a bill with amendments made in course of passage. Consider a Wisconsin case, *Ross v. Ebert* (1957). The 1945 Wisconsin legislature passed a Fair Employment Code directed against discrimination by reason of race. It was the legislature's first venture into this area of regulation, obviously an area of controversy that would present problems of implementation on which the state had no experience. As introduced, the bill empowered a state administrative agency to order violators to cease and desist, and gave the courts power to review and to enforce the agency's orders.

An amendment in course of passage struck out this enforcement provision and left only authorization to the agency to hold hearings, make findings, publicize the findings, and make recommendations to the interested parties to accept a suitable resolution of the matter. In 1951 and again in 1955, amendments restoring compulsory remedies were introduced but failed to pass. Against this record the Wisconsin court seems to have acted properly in denying a later suit which, drawing on the court's Equity powers, sought a mandatory injunction to enforce the Code. The succession of events had made convincingly clear that, venturing cautiously into a new and emotionally charged field of regulation, the legislature had purposely rejected sanctions other than the sanction of hearings, findings, and publicity.[28]

Courts are cautious in using materials from legislative history other than committee reports or the record of changes in the text of bills. Material beyond these points is likely to present sharper questions of credibility. Legislative hearings may produce detailed comments on pending bills, but typically these come from partisans of one interest or another and must be discounted accordingly. State legislatures generally do not keep records of floor debate, but Congress of course produces the *Congressional Record.* Debate there preserved is often fragmentary, subject to members' off-floor "amendment" of their remarks, and blurred by diversity of views which may go without ordered challenge or review. Thus it is not surprising to hear a Supreme Court opinion warning that "In construing laws we have been extremely wary of testimony before committee hearings and in debates on the floor of Congress save for precise analyses of statutory phrases by the sponsors of the proposed laws."[29]

Out of such concerns the Supreme Court—more by what it has done than through closely articulated doctrine—has indicated cautionary limits on reaching far into evidence from legislative hearings or debates. Where the Court has invoked material from hearings, most often it has been in defining the general purpose of a measure rather than its meaning in detail. On an occasion when the Court departed from this caution it was on stronger evidence than simply the statements of lobbyists. The Court gave special weight to remarks of a trade union spokesman in a Congressional hearing regarding the intent of a particular section of the Railway Labor Act. But it noted, as it had on prior occasions, that that Act "was, and was acknowledged to be, an agreement worked out between management and labor and ratified by the Congress and the President."[30]

In using recorded debate, the Court has distinguished between what was said on the floor by specialists on the pending bill or provision—members of the committee which considered the bill, members in charge of allocating the time limited for discussion under a rule of the chamber, or sponsors—and what was said by members who had no such special connection with shaping the measure. The Court will give weight to what the specialist members said, either on general purpose or on detailed content of the bill. But it is unlikely to regard isolated statements by generalist members, especially on matters of detailed meaning; probably the generalists' statements will have influence only when they make a fairly consistent pattern identifying the broad purposes of the proposal.[31] Judges are not invariably this cautious and sometimes press reliance on legislative history to a point that elicits objections from colleagues.[32] On the whole, however, the decisions approach the matter with commonsense appraisal of the credibility of the material.

The second type of recognition judges give to the process of producing legislation is the guidance they may find in the delineation of public policy through a succession of statutory provisions. There are matters to which legislators keep returning over the years. As they do so, they are likely to mark out the boundaries of policy more precisely or to indicate the intensity with which they hold certain objectives. The Supreme Court found persuasive evidence to such an effect in the record of Congress's successive dealings with an important element of federal court jurisdiction:

> From the beginning suits between citizens of different states, or involving federal questions, could neither be brought in the federal courts nor removed to them, unless the value of the matter

> in controversy was more than a specified amount. Pursuant to this policy the jurisdiction of federal courts of first instance has been narrowed by successive acts of Congress, which have progressively increased the jurisdictional amount. The policy of the statute calls for its strict construction. . . . Due regard for the rightful independence of state governments, which should actuate federal courts, requires that they scrupulously confine their own jurisdiction to the precise limits which the statute has defined.[33]

Judges also recognize that the content of public policy may grow by accretion of statutory precedents in a fashion analogous to the growth of common law. Statutes dealing with a variety of subjects may begin to cluster around some common value judgment. Recognizing this reality, a court is warranted in finding evidence of legislative intent under a given act by reference to what legislators have done regarding like subjects under other acts. Thus some decisions have given decisive weight to the fact that in dealing with similar substantive policies, legislators have adopted quite different procedural provisions; the judges drew the inference that they should not read in by implication a type of procedure omitted from one statute, though contained in others dealing with like subject matter.[34]

Given variety and change in the circumstances to which officials must apply legislation, a statute of broad reach is not a finished product the day the legislature adopts it. Thus where they find the meaning in some respect uncertain, judges will give weight to a sustained, consistent course of application of a statute, originating close to the date of enactment, by those charged with its administration, where the record shows no substantial legislative question or disavowal of the practice. Speaking for the Court, Justice Cardozo recognized that fulfillment of statutory policy was likely to require a continuing process of adjustment:

> True indeed it is that administrative practice does not avail to overcome a statute so plain in its commands as to leave nothing for construction. True it also is that administrative practice, consistent and generally unchallenged, will not be overturned except for very cogent reasons if the scope of the command is indefinite

> and doubtful. . . . . The practice has peculiar weight when it involves a contemporaneous construction of a statute by the men charged with the responsibility of setting its machinery in motion, of making the parts work efficiently and smoothly while they are yet untried and new.[35]

There is similar recognition of the process aspect of legislation in decisions that the rule-making power of agencies is not confined to power expressly granted. "Where the act uses ambiguous terms or is of doubtful construction, a clarifying regulation or one indicating the method of its application to specific cases not only is permissible but is to be given great weight by the courts."[36]

The sum of these several lines of doctrine and practice is plain: The statutory text is basic and central. But if law is to be a vital force in society, the text usually must be seen as part of a flow of policy-making activity that originates before the text is voted and continues after it is on the books.

FORM AND SUBSTANCE IN STATUTE LAW

Reaching a proper adjustment between regard for the forms of law and for the substance of its policy often poses hard problems in administering legal order. Tension between these elements is inherent in a constitutional legal order, which seeks to serve public interest within a structured disposition of official power. The interplay of a general statutory text and a particular situation, where contestants seek to use the statute to satisfy different interests, may present real or apparent collisions between respect for authoritative form on the one hand, and on the other, appeal to what a party argues to be the spirit or essence of the end that he believes the statute is intended to serve. Those who would properly apply a statute must seek to fulfill the substance of its policy within the framework of its text—an effort that calls for wisdom in not exalting either to exclusion of regard for the other.

The classic decision preferring substance over form remains *Church of the Holy Trinity v. United States* (1892).[37] The action was for a penalty set by an 1885 act of Congress which provided:

> That from and after the passage of this act it shall be unlawful for any person, company, partnership, or corporation, in any manner whatsoever, to prepay the transportation, or in any way assist or encourage the importation or migration of any alien or aliens, any foreigner or foreigners, into the United States, its Territories, or the District of Columbia, under contract or agreement, parol or special, express or implied, made previous to the importation or migration of such aliens, foreigner or foreigners, to perform labor or service of any kind in the United States, its Territories, or the District of Columbia.[38]

The church had made a contract with the Reverend E. Walpole Warren, an alien residing in England, by which he would move to New York City and become pastor of the church, which he thereafter did. The trial court held that the transaction fell within the statute's ban, and gave judgment for the United States. The Supreme Court reversed. The Supreme Court conceded that, item by item, the statute in terms applied to the situation. The church was a duly organized religious corporation. Warren was an alien. The contract, made prior to his leaving England, was a way to encourage his move. The contract was to perform service for the church within the United States. But the Court found that the case fell within "a familiar rule, that a thing may be within the letter of the statute and yet not within the statute, because not within its spirit, nor within the intention of its makers." From judicial notice of conditions in the labor market in the late nineteenth-century United States, from the focus of petitions and testimony presented before committees of Congress, and from the report of the Senate Committee on Education and Labor recommending passage of the bill, the Court concluded that Congress intended only to prohibit contractors from recruiting abroad great numbers of cheap, unskilled manual labor, depressing the level of wages in the United States. "It was never suggested that we had in this country a surplus of brain toilers, and, least of all, that the market for the services of Christian ministers was depressed by foreign competition. Those were matters to which the attention of Congress, or of the people, was not directed." In addition to these factors immediately related to passage of the bill, the Court also noted the long-standing official policy in favor of organized religion, manifest in documents stretching from the Mayflower Compact through colonial charters to provisions of the Federal and State constitutions and other legal declarations. From this chain of policy it concluded that, beyond the specific legislative history it cited, "no purpose of action against religion can be imputed to any legislation, state or national, because this is a religious people. This is historically true."[39]

It would be simplistic to read this as a decision only against mechanical literalism. The ruling is a stronghanded treatment of a statutory text that was clear and sweeping. The Supreme Court conceded the breadth of the text, which used generic terms (for example, "labor or service of any kind"). Moreover, the text hammered at alternatives in a fashion suggesting that Congress feared calculated efforts to circumvent its policy and wanted to cast a wide net against such contrivances (as in the reference to contracts "parol or special, express or implied"). The Court's opinion makes resolution of the issue seem easier than it is, by ignoring the textual implications against evasion. After all, the federal circuit court below had found a violation of the act. Certainly the Supreme Court's decision and many rulings following it offer considerable freedom for judges to prefer what they deem to be the substantive ends of a statute over its text.[40]

Church of the Holy Trinity notwithstanding, one cannot read many judicial opinions interpreting statutes without realizing that ordinarily courts give prime weight to the statutory text. This practice appropriately recognizes the distinguishing formal character of statute law as compared with common law. Lawyers and judges find the definition of a proposition of common law in inferences and trends of policy indicated by doctrinal analysis and holdings in a succession of precedents; it inheres in the common law process that boundaries and specifications have no single definitive expression. The special character of legislation is the presence of a formally defined text, providing the authoritative base and framework within which all who would resort to the statute must operate. Even the iconoclastic Professor Radin conceded that

> the necessity of considering precise words points to an important difference when a statute is to be applied, and imposes certain limitations in the application. Whether words be the skin of an idea, in the simile of Mr. Justice Holmes, or chameleons which take their color from their surroundings, in the figure occasionally used by Continental jurists, the skin, we must remember, is already half filled; the chameleon's natural gray shines through the red and green which it has assumed from its surroundings.[41]

However, courts' recognition of the distinctive deference owing to the words in the statute book is sometimes veiled. Lawyers need to train themselves to see the full range within which judges react to the influence of the statutory text.

Courts respect the formal text by acknowledging that it provides the ultimate frame of reference within which a given situation must fall if the matter is to be governed by the statute. As the Supreme Court conceded, the Church of the Holy Trinity could not escape the statute by claiming that what the Church had done could not be brought within the broad frame set by the text. But cases do arise where the situation in issue simply cannot be brought within the outermost limits set by the words in the statute book. In 1872 the Wisconsin court held that a 1707 English statute which relieved of liability for harm from escape of fire any person "in whose house or chamber any fire shall accidentally begin" did not furnish a defense to a railroad sued for damages from fire started by sparks from its locomotive. The ruling was clearly correct; railroad operations presented a situation wholly outside the field of concern defined by the statutory text.[42]

Courts commonly give potent effect to the statutory text by using it to assign the burden of persuasion between contestants who would read the act differently. The point is important. Often the allocation of the burden of persuading the court of the intent of the legislature has the effect of determining who wins and who loses; the party who must carry the burden may not be able to sustain it. Judges do not usually make the point explicit, perhaps because they think it follows so logically from the presence of an authoritative text to apportion burdens of persuasion between the parties. Thus here, again, lawyers need some skill in reading between the lines of judicial opinions to identify precisely what courts are doing.

In *Church of the Holy Trinity* the Supreme Court implies that the burden of persuasion is on the defendant. The opinion concedes "that the act of the corporation is within the letter of this section," notes that "Not only are the general words labor and service both used; but also, as it were to guard against any narrow interpretation and emphasize a breadth of meaning, to them is added 'of any kind'; and, further, as noticed by the Circuit Judge in his opinion, the fifth section, which makes specific exceptions, among them professional actors, artists, lecturers, singers and domestic servants, strengthens the idea that every other kind of labor and service was intended to be reached by the first section." The Court grants that "there is great force to this reasoning." When, thereafter, it nonetheless rejects the government's interpretation, it does so by finding it rebutted from material derived from judicial notice, from the legislative history of the Act, and from the general public policy favoring religious organizations manifest in a long succession of constitutional and statutory provisions. The overall tone of the analysis is that the statutory text cast the burden of persuasion on the defendant, and the defendant met that burden.[43] The effect given the formal text in allocating the burden of persuasion is the more striking because the Court here deals with a penal statute. By a familiar canon, if they find reasonable doubt of the meaning of a penal statute, judges should resolve the doubt in favor of the defendant. But where the text is emphatically broad, courts without mentioning strict construction of penal statutes often find the defendant within the coverage of the act if he has not brought forth persuasive evidence to the contrary.[44]

The opinion in *United States v. Trans-Missouri Freight As-*

nd they will give weight to sustained, consistent, unchal- l practical construction of the act by those charged with ng it out.

: willingness of twentieth-century courts in the United to give weight to such materials outside the statute books in sharp contrast to English doctrine.[49] English judges evidence of legislative hearings and debates altogether, se they rule it legally incompetent evidence of legislative ; they allow no scope for admitting or excluding such ial on judgments of its credibility, but simply refuse to look t all. They make one qualification: they will take account :ts of history properly subject to judicial notice, to show general circumstances existed to bring about a statute.[50] mparison of doctrine on this matter in England and in this try brings into relief some underlying value questions. To ccustomed to the pragmatic flexibility with which courts : United States use materials extrinsic to the statute book, nglish rule seems at first rigid, doctrinaire, and possibly a . for judges' distaste for acknowledging the supremacy of ament. The modern English rule may seem out of tune the old precepts of *Heydon's Case*, which treat statutory y as the product of a continuing process of lawmaking. But *lon's Case* probably stands close to current English doctrine; actors it emphasizes regard legislation in the light of prior mon law and the known history of the times.[51]

iere are sound reasons for caution in looking beyond the te book for evidence of the legislature's intention. Sepa- n of powers values are at stake. Short of constitutional lim- ns, the legislature is entitled to set public policy. The words tes onto the statute book are its prime means and its delib- ly chosen means to define policy and to confer authority impose limitations on others who will translate policy into icular action.[52] The economics of everyday administration gal order normally require that people act on the basis of r reasonable reading of the statute books; costs in time and iey preclude lawyers from looking past the text to search scripts of committee hearings or committee reports every

sociation (1897) provides another leading example of the influence of a statutory text in allocating the burden of persuasion on legislative intent. As usual, the allocation is implicit rather than explicit, but it is nonetheless there. In sweeping terms the Sherman Act declares illegal every contract or conspiracy in restraint of trade among the states. Significantly, the Supreme Court did not pose the issue before it as whether the government had shown that the Act covered rate fixing agreements among interstate railroads, but whether the defendants had made a persuasive case that Congress did not intend to cover them. The Court noted that railroad counsel "urged that the debates in Congress show beyond a doubt that the act as passed does not include railroads." Examining the legislative history presented by the defendants, the Court found it inconclusive: "All that can be determined from the debates and reports is that various members had various views, and we are left to determine the meaning of this act, as we determine the meaning of other acts, from the language used therein." The Court was also prepared to consider the Act in light of "the history of the times," of which it might take judicial notice. But it framed its treatment of this source, also, in negative rather than positive terms, indicating that it was not the government's responsibility to show by judicial notice that railroads were intended to be included, but the responsibility of the railroads to show that they were not included: "A reference to this history of the times does not, as we think, furnish us with any strong reason for believing that it was only trusts that were in the minds of the members of Congress, and that railroads and their manner of doing business were wholly excluded therefrom."[45]

Judges also frequently command respect for the statutory text by declaring that its "plain meaning" must govern. However, we encounter the formula often in contexts where it seems invoked to avoid acknowledging judges' policy preferences. We are entitled to regard it with some skepticism as a reliable canon of judicial self-restraint.

Church of the Holy Trinity demonstrates a basic qualification to the respect for "plain meaning"—that deference to the statutory text does not require automatically governing by the text every situation that the words taken by themselves are capable of embracing. As I have just pointed out, this qualification can coexist with deference to the text as allocating the burden of persuasion as to legislative intent. The caution is only that we should not regard the statute's words as exacting some mechanical response from those to whom it may apply.[46]

This is a caution that fits two interlocked realities of legislative process to which the Supreme Court in effect responded. Legislatures are pragmatically-minded bodies, their members typically pressed by more business than they have time to handle, buffeted by competing outside interests, as practicing politicians never far from the thought of reelection and the bearing on reelection of the positions they take. They never sit to pass laws out of a planned design to create a single, comprehensive scheme of legal order. Only rarely and after unusual, sustained activity by interested groups do they adopt systematized patterns of law for broad sectors of community life, such as the Uniform Commercial Code. Normally they act for limited, or at least specialized ends. The legislative process is cumbersome; inertia or delay figure more easily in it than the pain of choosing policy; normally legislatures act only when outside interests exert effective pressure on them to do something. Thus there is realism behind the Court's announcement in the *Church* case that a proper guide to Congress's intent "is found in the evil which [the statute] . . . is designed to remedy; and for this the court properly looks at contemporaneous events, the situation as it existed, and as it was pressed upon the attention of the legislative body."

Since the evidence of the hearings and the report of a legislative committee showed that it was the importation of cheap, unskilled labor that troubled those who wanted the statute, the realities of legislative process point to the conclusion that there was probably no intent of Congress to deal with a wholly different matter, the entry of "brain toilers".[47] This is not an analysis that requires unquestioning acceptance. The breadth of the

statutory text, the use of generic term
of alternative phrasing suggest that Co
to cast a wide net to prevent evasion o
of including some situations that Con
on their own merits. In this light ther
for the trial court's decision that the A
But the Supreme Court's interpretati
pragmatism characteristic of the legisla
carries persuasion.

Courts in this country qualify the de
statutory text by their willingness to us
the text to establish legislative intent—
stipulate, that those who would invoke t
show that the text, taken by itself, is unc
aspects of this doctrine—acceptance of s
and requirement of prior demonstratio
ing—raise questions of principle and of

The earlier discussion noted that ou
legislation is the product of a law-maki
for example, by records of legislative he
ports of legislative committees, and com
introduced bills and of amendments co
of passage. Few rules of competence lim
legislative intent outside of the statute b
use only evidence generated by those eng
sidering a bill. Normally the evidence m
both prior to and contemporaneous with
later lawsuit courts will not admit a legisla
intent with which he participated in pas
practice establishes qualifications on this
both, however, within the norm of resort
erated by those involved in official procee
from the norm of giving weight to legislati
temporaneous with the enactment by the
praise the statute before them also in the lig
or prior legislative proceedings on the same

time they must advise clients of their rights or duties under a statute.[53] Ready resort to legislative history may increase the effects of unequal resources among contending parties; wealthy clients can better afford to pay for lawyers' time in searching beyond the statute books, and in any case those who live near the limited number of libraries that hold legislative documents will enjoy advantages denied to those at a distance.[54] We must weigh such elements, too, with the fact that documented legislative history may not be reliable. Cross-currents of contending interests in the legislative arena may distort or confuse the record, perhaps partly by intentional effort of partisans of a particular cause to manufacture evidence to their interest.[55] Reasons of justice as well as of efficiency argue that we should give great weight to the statutory text against material beyond the text.

Judges in the United States routinely stipulate that before they will consider evidence of legislative intent outside the words of the statute they must be persuaded that the words taken in themselves are of uncertain meaning. They commonly declare this rule with a finality that appears to make it a test of the competence of any extrinsic evidence: "If the language be clear it is conclusive. There can be no construction where there is nothing to construe."[56] One might argue that if the statutory text points one way and reports of legislative committees that considered the measure point another, the text can hardly be deemed clear. But the standard rule obviously will not allow this argument, for the rule makes a showing of uncertainty on the face of the statute an absolute prerequisite to looking beyond the face. If we accept the standard rule at face value its logic is compelling: "In proper cases, . . . [legislative] committee reports are given consideration in determining the meaning of a statute, but only where that meaning is doubtful. They cannot be resorted to for the purpose of construing a statute contrary to the natural import of its terms. . . . Like other extrinsic aids to construction their use is 'to solve, but not to create an ambiguity.'"[57]

However, judicial practice is not as rigid as the formula. In the opinion I have just quoted, having sternly put aside as incompetent evidence two committee reports which the opinion conceded flatly stated the contrary of the interpretation the Supreme Court now adopted, the Court went on to bulwark its decision by invoking another type of extrinsic evidence, from administrative construction of the Act.[58] Time and again, having found the statutory text plain on its face, opinions nonetheless consider evidence outside the text. In practice judges are likely to examine text and extrinsic materials together, treating use of extrinsic evidence relative to the text as presenting a question of credibility and not of competence.[59] Justice Holmes states the working reality: "It is said that when the meaning of language is plain we are not to resort to evidence in order to raise doubts. That is rather an axiom of experience than a rule of law, and does not preclude consideration of persuasive evidence if it exists."[60]

To treat with merited skepticism the conventional prerequisite of showing uncertainty in the text before going outside it does not negate the value of the formula. The formula serves the proper separation of powers principle so far as it provides a persistent reminder to those who must apply statutes that the legislature is entitled to set the frame of public policy, and that the text it votes into the statute books is its most positive and deliberate exercise of that function.

RULES OF CONSTRUCTION

As Reports of appellate court decisions multiplied from the early nineteenth century, judges in the United States invoked an impressive array of rules of construction in aid of finding legislative intent. Some rules had enough basis in ordinary patterns of communication or in realities of legislative process to provide sensible guidelines where statutory words did not by their immediate force resolve all issues. If judges were faithful to the limits of their role under the separation of powers, they treated even the most sensible rules as indicators and not as mandates. A rule of construction was only an aid to fulfilling the legislature's intent; as such it was always rebuttable by more specific matter from the statutory text or from legislative history.[61] Some rules were so vague or offered such facile justifications for contradictory outcomes that they served more to cloak unavowed value premises of those who used them than to help fulfill the legislature's objectives.[62]

By the late twentieth century many rules familiar in nineteenth-century opinions and treatises had atrophied or suffered sharply diminished appeal. My concern is with a few which survive in action and continue to figure materially in current handling of statutes. Two main lines of difference emerge. Some rules of construction endure because they reflect specific realities of communication through the legislative process. Most rules inherited from the nineteenth century were of a highly general character. This is the type that has tended to disappear in twentieth-century analysis. Of this kind there are only two notable survivors—the rule enjoining strict construction of statutes in derogation of common law, and the rule requiring strict construction of penal statutes.

The rules of construction that best reflect the realities of legislative process are those that are most consistent with the deference owed the legislature's primacy in policymaking. Three types of rules creating presumptions as to legislative intent especially conform to this attitude: those dealing with word usage, with statutory context, and with legislation bearing on related subjects.

Legislators do not usually invent language; like other people normally they draw on the common stock of communication. Most of the time it is realistic to presume that they intend to follow familiar usage. One basic distinction in regular usage is that between words that connote broad classes of persons, things or situations and those that denote particular items. Thus where a statute uses generic rather than specific words there seems reason to presume that the legislature intends an expansive rather than a restrictive reading. In *Church of the Holy Trinity*, though it found the inferences from the face of the statute rebutted from legislative history, the Supreme Court conceded that there was "great force" to the argument for breadth from the words of the Act. The Act did not forbid the assisted emigration of foreigners to perform carpentry, shoemaking, or any other particular occupations, but rather, the Court noted, "the general words labor and service [are] both used."[63] In contrast, the Court gave full force to what it deemed words of broad categories in holding that the federal Safety Appliance Acts required power brakes on a motor track car used by a section gang in maintaining the railroad right of way: Congress "wrote into the Safety Appliance Acts that their coverage embraced 'all trains, locomotives, tenders, cars, and similar vehicles.' This plain language could not have been more all-inclusive. This Court has construed the language of the Act in its generic sense."[64]

Another presumption with a realistic basis in regular patterns of communication says that if the legislature uses words which have an ordinary meaning, we should assume that it intends them in that meaning unless the contrary is shown. The burden of persuasion is on one who claims that the words should be read in some sense peculiar to a special situation, as with usage particular to a given trade or category of technical or professional knowledge. Thus where a tariff act fixed different rates for "vegetables" and for "fruits" without indicating any specialized meaning for the terms, the Supreme Court appealed to common usage to decide that Congress did not intend to tax tomatoes as "fruit."[65]

However, with all its commonsense appeal, resort to the ordinary meaning of words carries a high risk of begging the real issue in many cases. Words do not have meaning in the abstract. They have meaning with reference only to some subject which those choosing the words mean to address. We cannot answer the question, what is the ordinary meaning of the word "ring" without asking a prior question: Is the speaker talking about a signal from a telephone, an ornament to slip on a finger, an arena under a circus tent? Often the difficult problem is to identify the subject the legislature intends to deal with; if we know that, then the ordinary meaning of the words, used with reference to that subject, is likely to present no serious issue. The majority opinion in *Caminetti v. United States* (1917) shows a classic instance of begging the true question under the deceptive simplicity of appealing to the presumption favoring ordinary meaning. The Mann Act makes it an offense knowingly to transport in interstate commerce any woman "for the purpose of prostitution or debauchery, or for any other immoral purpose." The defendant took a woman across a state line for illicit sex, without payment. The majority had no trouble in finding his conduct within the ban of the Act:

> While such immoral purpose would be more culpable in morals and attributed to baser motives if accompanied with the expectation of pecuniary gain, such considerations do not prevent the lesser offense against morals of furnishing transportation in order that a woman may be debauched, or become a mistress or a concubine from being the execution of purposes within the meaning of this law. To say the contrary would shock the common understanding of what constitutes an immoral purpose when those terms are applied, as here, to sexual relations."[66]

But the fighting issue was precisely whether Congress used the words intending to deal with "sexual relations" or only with commercialized sexual relations. When Congress passed the Mann Act there was unquestionably a "common understanding of what constitutes an immoral purpose", when people were talking about any sexual relations outside of marriage.[67] But that fact provides no evidence whether the subject Congress was addressing was all illicit sex or only illicit sex for pay.[68]

A third presumption that fits the realities of legislative communication is that which enjoins that we read particular words or phrases in the light cast by other parts of the same statute. Legislation of any consequence is typically a complex of parts. It will have components that deal with persons or situations regulated, with the nature of apprehended evils or needs, with goals and the ranking of goals, and with procedures or means to accomplish its objectives. Adjustments, bargains, compromises made in hammering out the final product will likely have explicit or implicit reflections in the different elements built into the statute. We should not romanticize the process of obtaining legislation; it is usually a somewhat rough-and-tumble business, and what emerges is unlikely to be a finely joined piece of cabinet work. Nonetheless, those who draft and shepherd through a measure create some pattern of policy, so that there is ground for presuming that their intent in particulars lies in the relations of those particulars to the surrounding pattern.[69]

The presence of an exception clause may provide an especially revealing example of the guides which context may provide. That there is an exception points up two aspects of the pattern of policy. First, it indicates that the legislature's attention was markedly focused on that aspect of the statute with which the exception deals; the matter involved was not treated casually or overlooked. Second, the substance of the exception is likely to put in sharper relief the contours of the principal policy. Consider *Gooch v. United States* (1935).[70] A federal statute made it an offense knowingly to transport in interstate commerce "any person who shall have been unlawfully seized, confined, inveigled, decoyed, kidnapped, abducted, or carried away by any means whatsoever and held for ransom or reward or otherwise, except, in the case of a minor, by a parent thereof." To avoid arrest, defendants resisted and disarmed police officers and forcibly carried them by car from Texas to Oklahoma, freeing them in Oklahoma. The defendants argued that the statute did not apply, because they had not acted for monetary gain. In rejecting their position the Supreme Court found that the exception clause was one factor that underlined the intended sweep of the Act, as covering kidnapping for any benefit sought by the kidnapper. The presence of the exception showed that Congress gave attention specifically to the matter of the kidnapper's objective. Moreover, the content of the exception was significant: "The words 'except, in case of a minor, by a parent thereof' emphasize the intended result of the enactment. They indicate legislative understanding that in their absence a parent, who carried his child away because of affection, might subject himself to condemnation of the statute."[71] The exception was highly specific and unusual in character. If, but for the exception, the statute would there apply, Congress must intend its basic text to have an extremely broad reach.

A fourth presumption belonging to the general category of rules which carry persuasion because they reflect characteristic legislative operations is that which, in reading the statute immediately in issue, gives weight to material contained in other acts dealing with the same subject or with similar subject matter.[72] A legislature typically acts only when and as someone presses it to act. Hence it is likely to deal at one point of time with less than the whole, potential extent of the issues or choices it confronts. Thus legislative intent may emerge in full definition only through a succession of acts.

So in *Gooch v. United States*, the Court gave weight to the fact that the phrase "for ransom or reward or otherwise" had not stood in that form in the kidnapping statute as Congress first enacted it. Had that been the original phrasing, the defendants might have pressed a familiar rule of construction, that the general words "or otherwise" should be read as intended to cover only such conduct as that indicated by the preceding, more specific words, and hence be taken as limited to kidnapping for some economic gain. The argument might have gained weight because, defendants would argue, as a penal statute the Act in case of doubt should be construed in their favor. But as first enacted in 1932 the statute only penalized kidnapping "for ransom or reward." In 1934 Congress took the trouble to amend the act to add "or otherwise", plus the narrow exception for parents. Given the cost of moving Congress to action, we should be slow to read "or otherwise" in a way that would rob it of distinctive force: "informed by experience during two years, and for reasons satisfactory to itself, Congress undertook by the 1934 Act to enlarge the earlier one and to clarify its purpose."[73]

In analogous fashion, when the Supreme Court was asked to rule that the Motor Carrier Act, 1935, empowered the Interstate Commerce Commission to fix reasonable qualifications and maximum hours of work of motor carrier employees other than those whose duties affected safety of operations, it drew its interpretation in part from the indications of federal legislation dealing with other forms of transport. It rejected the broader reading of the 1935 Act because, so read, it would give the Commission authority "quite distinct from the settled practice of Congress. That policy has been consistent in legislating for such regulation of transportation employees in matters of movement and safety only. The Hours of Service Act imposes restrictions on the hours of labor of employees 'actually engaged in or connected with the movement of any train.' The Seamen's Act limits employee regulations under it to members of ships' crews. The Civil Aeronautics Authority has authority over hours of service of employees 'in the interest of safety.'" Moreover, there was uncontradicted documentation that "at the time of the passage of the Motor Vehicle Act 'forty states had regulatory measures relating to the hours of service of employees' and every one 'applied exclusively to drivers or helpers on the vehicles.'"[74]

Judges' readiness to give weight to inferences from the succession of statutory provisions on the same subject or to provisions in other legislation dealing with like subject matter accords with their willingness to take note of amendments dealt with in the course of passage of a bill, and to consider evidence from committee reports, and transcripts of legislative hearings and debates. Arguably, material drawn from what legislators vote into the statute books should be preferred evidence of likely legislative intent; the fact of its enactment carries more persuasive certification of its validity. At least, the tone of judicial opinions is to treat such statute book evidence with respect comparable to that accorded committee reports.

In contrast to rules of construction that reflect familiar patterns of communication or operations in the legislative process are those that explicitly declare broad value preferences not tied to any particular statutory subject matter. What stands out in the rule (presumption) that a statute in derogation of common law should be construed as not intended to change common law unless that intent is made plain is the abstract character of the proposition. By the terms of the rule it does not matter whether the statute deals with rights of personality or of property, with land title or liability for negligent behavior. If a given interpretation of the act would change existing common law, the presumption is against that interpretation. The same applies to the doctrine that in case of doubt we should construe a penal statute so as to favor the accused. In its ordinary form, the rule is stated as one of strict construction of penal statutes. The conventional statement is too narrow, measured against what courts in fact do when they apply the rule, which is to adopt either a restrictive or an extensive reading of the statutory text, whichever will favor the accused. In any event, according to the standard formula it does not matter whether the statute deals with invasion of security of person or property, with conduct offensive to long-standing canons of community morality (theft or infliction of bodily harm), or with conduct newly defined as deviating from standards of proper marketing behavior (misrepresentation of quality of goods). If a given interpretation would mean a penalty on the accused, we are to give the accused the benefit of the doubt.

The abstract character of these rules is highlighted by the nature of the formal option open to the party who would escape their application. Judges sometimes speak as though the rule of strict construction of statutes in derogation of common law imposed procedural limits on the exercise of legislative power, requiring explicit statements of intent to change the older law, or operating as an analogue of the doctrine that a statute might offend due process standards because it was too vague.[75] However, generally it is clear that these rules raise only presumptions as to legislative intent, and as such are rebuttable. Nonetheless, even in this tempered form the rules might materially affect the relative situation of the contending parties. One who would oppose application of such a rule must counter its abstraction with concrete, particularized demonstration of a different policy manifest in legislative history. Obviously his position is the more at risk because he must carry this burden, which he may not be able to meet.[76] Meanwhile his opponent enjoys the protection of a doctrine that he can invoke on a minimal showing, requiring no demonstration of a public policy specific to the situation with which the legislation dealt.[77]

A valid objection to the abstract character of these rules of construction is that they are likely to veil unacknowledged value preferences which may not stand close examination. Especially in older decisions one senses that sometimes judges, conscious and proud of their leading role in the nineteenth century as makers of common law on a grand scale, invoked such rules of construction because they regarded the growth of statute law as an intrusion on their importance and their superior professional skill in building policy.[78] The twentieth-century temper has changed in this respect, as Justice Jackson observed, speaking for the Supreme Court in a 1943 decision:

> Some rules of statutory construction come down to us from sources that were hostile toward the legislative process itself and thought it generally wise to restrict the operation of an act to its narrowest possible compass. However well these rules may serve at times to aid in deciphering legislative intent, they long have been subordinated to the doctrine that courts will construe the details of an act in conformity with its dominating general purpose, will read text in the light of context and will interpret the text so far as the meaning of the words fairly permits so as to carry out in particular cases the generally expressed legislative policy.[79]

On occasion restrictive construction of penal statutes or of statutes argued to change common law may serve proper public policy. A court may presume against intent to change some doctrine of common law because the judges find sufficient explanation for a broad statutory text in one particular focus, and in effect recognize the normal reality that legislative process centers on one problem at a time.[80] Their restrictive interpretation of expansive language may be an unavowed application of the familiar rule of construing legislation to avoid a serious issue of constitutionality, where the reach of the act might offend due process standards because of vagueness.[81] Where legislation forbids conduct of a kind which in many contexts general community norms would accept as socially useful, as in the ordinary marketing of goods and services, courts are likely to give the benefit of doubt as to the statute's meaning to the accused. In contrast, where a statute penalizes conduct—theft, for example, or sale of liquor to minors—which is either clearly condemned or at least treated with great distrust by general community standards, judges are likely to apply the statutory text in its full sweep, and probably will not mention the rule of strict construction of penal statutes, let alone trouble to state evidence or arguments to rebut its application.[82] In some situations, thus, resort to these abstract rules of construction may serve a legitimate interest. But it accords better with the twentieth-century temper of legal administration that such particular value preferences as the rules may serve should be brought under open examination, for the legitimacy as well as the predictability of law.

If we regard together uses judges make of statutory text, legislative history, and general rules of construction in the second half of the twentieth century, one approach is clearly dominant, standing in sharp contrast to nineteenth-century treatment of legislation. The twentieth-century emphasis is on coming to a specific focus on a given statute in its full-dimensioned particularity of policy, rather than emphasizing material or values not immediately connected to that enactment. Courts now seem usually to strive to grasp the distinctive message of statutory words, taken in their own context, with reference to the documented process that produced that particular act, including legislative history deserving credibility, and policy guides supplied by the legislature's successive development of the given policy area and related areas. The twentieth-century emphasis thus is not on broad, standardized formulas, but on custom-built determinations, fashioned out of materials immediate and special to the legislation at issue. It is an approach both more pragmatic and more deferential to the functions of courts under the separation of powers. For our time the single most practical guide to the interpretation of statutes is a caution from Justice Holmes, that "every question of construction is unique, and an argument that would prevail in one case may be inadequate in another."[83]

3

THE CONSTITUTIONALITY OF STATUTES

Some tension is inherent in relations among three elements of our legal system that center on the legislative branch. One, the norm is that elected, representative assemblies shall be the principal agencies to declare general public policy. Two, but they are to do this within grants and limits contained in constitutions. In some measure judges share with legislators and executives responsibility for holding legislation within bounds set by constitutional standards and rules. Three, in some degree tension is inescapable between constitutional grants and limits, whose function is to provide an enduring frame of authority, and the currents of legislative response to ongoing needs and wants and to changing circumstances in the society. The range, variety, and differing intensities of human relations and interests, and the insistent pressures of change in physical, biological, and social contexts mean that strain between constitutional structure and legislative adjustments can never be finally resolved by some definitive code. The system works only by developing and observing procedures of comity among those who hold differing roles in fashioning public policy but who share responsibility for maintaining the constitutional frame.

This essay examines key procedures for achieving the necessary adjustments between constitutional grants and limits and exercise of legislative will and choice in making particular public policy. My concern here is not primarily with substantive constitutional law, but with the criteria and procedures developed to deal with special problems involved in analyzing, briefing, arguing, or deciding questions about the constitutionality of legislative action. Most of these criteria and procedures center on, or qualify, the "presumption of constitutionality."

Much working constitutional law has been embodied chiefly in legislative and executive practice. Development of the fiscal power of the national government offers a notable example. In his Report on the Subject of Manufactures (1791) Hamilton asserted that the power of Congress to spend money raised by using its power to tax was a distinct head of Congressional authority and not merely auxiliary to other grants of power; in his view wherever spending by the national government could reasonably be deemed to promote a national public interest, Congress was empowered to spend, apart from whatever goals it might pursue under other powers the Constitution particularly gave it. Not until a calculated dictum in 1936 did the Supreme Court stamp its approval on Hamilton's proposition. But between 1791 and 1936—not without some intervening controversy—Congress built a course of appropriations precedent that in practice demonstrated Hamilton's reading of the Constitution.[1]

In this mode legislators—and chief executives as participants in legislative process—have been more given to putting content into constitutional law by framing and considering particular bills and voting on them than by expounding the theory of what they regard as their constitutional authority. In our tradition explanation of the steps taken toward decision has been the special responsibility of judges. Thus most procedural doctrine dealing with techniques of comity in handling questions of the constitutionality of statutes comes from judges, and most of it from the United States Supreme Court. This essay draws mainly from what that Court has given us. However, the guidelines that the Court has supplied are relevant to all those—lawyers, executive and administrative officers, legislators, laymen who must make their own decisions affected by what they find in the statute books—whose interests and needs require that they weigh the validity of what legislatures have done.[2]

For my present purpose I pass by the long debated question of whether judicial review of the constitutionality of statutes is legitimate within our tradition of republican government, under which popularly elected assemblies are the prime bodies to determine the substance of general public policy. Accepting judicial review as a material element of our operating legal order, I inquire how we have gone about trying to make it work. However, even in this limited context the issue of legitimacy of judicial review does not disappear. There is persisting unease about the relation of judicial review to the proper role of representative bodies, regularly responsible to broadly defined electorates. This continued unease is at the root of the special procedures our experience has evolved for handling issues of the constitutionality of statutes. Indeed, the strength which the Supreme Court has given the presumption of constitutionality over a wide range of legislation in the late twentieth century reflects a bad conscience of judges regarding the extent of judicial policymaking wielded in the past in the name of substantive due process and equal protection of law.[3]

INSTITUTIONAL ROLES OF LEGISLATORS AND JUDGES

Three factors have shaped distinctive institutional roles for legislators and judges, and special procedures for dealing with questions of the validity of statutes, under constitutional grants and limitations. These factors are (1) the difference between first-line and secondary responsibility for the content of public policy, (2) the range of determinations legislators must make (whether explicitly or implicitly) if they operate with at least a workable minimum of rationality in passing statutes, and (3) the different tasks presented to legislators and judges under highly general provisions (constitutional standards) and under more particularized provisions (constitutional rules).

Originating and Reviewing Policy. When a member introduces a bill, or when a legislative chamber directs one of its committees to investigate a matter which may concern the public interest, the action puts legislators on the front line of contact between legal processes and currents of life outside those processes. The legislators' position on that front line may be thrown into further relief by legislative hearings where proponents of a measure stage-manage their presentation, or competing interests joust for position. Legislators rarely originate proposals. But when others exert effective pressure for or against action, legislators inescapably make the first official determinations whether or not and on what terms they will translate into statute law the issues thrown up out of the community life. Where no statute governs, and parties press judges to employ public power in behalf of one value or another, courts in making common law originate policy; they then stand on the front line of contact between law and the life of society moving around and about the law. But, asked to pass on the constitutionality of a statute, a court is a reviewing body, not an originator of policy. Here another responsible legal agency has already passed at first hand and by immediate contact on a problem and has made formal response. Moreover, the presence of the statute means that the problem has already been sifted through the processes of the agency—the legislature—which our separation of powers tradition declares to be the prime instrument for determining the particular substance of public policy.[4]

Judge Learned Hand provides the best statement in reported decisions of courts of the principle that in dealing with a challenge to the constitutionality of a statute the judge's role should normally be that of a reviewer and not originator of policy. Full elaboration of this principle has been surprisingly recent. It was as late as 1935 that Judge Hand spelled out the full scope of the distinction between legislative and judicial functions in this context:

> We are indeed all familiar with the doctrine that a court will not [when it undertakes to determine whether a statute violates the 'due process' clause] . . . substitute its own opinion of what conduces best to the public welfare; there is a large demesne in which the legislative choice between conflicting social values is final, and courts undertake to intervene only when it appears beyond

> peradventure that that choice has not been defensible. All this is hornbook law and needs no citation; but as far as we can find, the question comes up for the first time whether when the court has undertaken an inquiry as to the facts on which the validity of a statute turns, the result is dependent upon its decision in the same sense as the result of an ordinary suit. If it finds to its own satisfaction that the necessary facts do not exist, is the law invalid? Or must it go further as in the case of the choice of values, and find not only that the facts did not exist, but that reasonable people could not believe that they did?. . . . It seems to us that there can be no doubt that the second is the only tolerable doctrine. Otherwise the legislature's power would in effect be merely to enact general hypothetical propositions, which would become imperative only in case courts concluded that the facts on which their applicability depended, actually existed. That is certainly not the traditional limit of a legislature's powers, frequently it institutes elaborate inquiry to learn the truth, just as it did in this case. The inquiry and its result are a part of its function, as exempt from judicial review as its social choices. If it has proceeded by commission or the like, the result may be more impressive, but it need not so proceed, and courts are as much bound in the one case as in the other. Therefore it is not necessary for the [supporters of the challenged statute] . . . to demonstrate the truth of the . . . findings [on which the legislature based its enactment], although incidentally we think that they are true. The relevant inquiry as to each is not what the master or we, or even the Supreme Court, may think the truth to have been, but whether reasonable people might have taken the view of the legislature. For this reason findings favorable to the statute are in substance conclusive, even if we should not ourselves agree with them; for they prove that the legislature in assuming the truth of what they declare, at least had reasonable warrant, and that, as we have said, is enough, just as it is in the case of a verdict, or the findings of an administrative tribunal.[5]

As Judge Hand indicates, a division of function and responsibility between originating and reviewing bodies is not unique to judicial review of the constitutionality of legislation. We more commonly encounter this distinction when a litigant asks a judge to set aside the verdict of a jury in a civil case; the judge should not set aside the verdict simply because he would not assess the evidence as the jury did, but only if he finds that no reasonable jurors could have found so. Similarly, called on to pass on the validity of findings and determinations by an administrative agency, the court is not to reject what the agency did because on the record made before the agency the court would find and order differently; the court is entitled to overturn the agency action only if the judges find no reasonable basis for it.[6]

These role differences derive from criteria of efficiency and of the proper separation of powers. Where a responsible body has already confronted evidence and competition or adjustment of diverse values in a firsthand, close examination, it would be wasteful to duplicate its effort. Read in the light of long-established tradition, constitutional guarantees of jury trial assign to jurors substantial scope for resolving issues of fact, and to some extent issues of fact-enmeshed values; to protect litigants and the morale of juries, judges should respect the jury's prerogative.[7] Legislatures today hold acknowledged constitutional authority to delegate powers to executive and administrative agencies. Twentieth-century legislative practice assigns to the legislature's delegates substantial scope for exercising judgment and building detailed programs by experience; respectful of the legislature's primacy in marking out broad policy, courts should respect the discretion that legislative practice indicates the legislature wants its executive or administrative agents to have.[8]

Of course both policy originators and policy reviewers owe respect to constitutional grants and limitations. But their responsibilities differ. Judges are not alone in swearing to uphold the constitutions under which they operate. Confronting with obvious asperity an issue that he felt the state legislature should not have created for himself and his colleagues, Justice Rosenberry commented for the Wisconsin Supreme Court,

> It would seem that [prior] decisions could not make plainer the fact that any law which prohibits the manufacture and sale of uncolored oleomargarine violates the constitution of the United States and of the state of Wisconsin. In this connection we are moved to observe that the mandates of the constitution are just

> as binding upon the conscience of the legislator as upon the conscience of the judge. The constitution is the mandate of a sovereign people to its servants and representatives, and no one of them has a right to ignore or disregard its plain commands. Every officer, legislative and executive as well as judicial, is required by the constitution, as a condition of holding his office, to take a solemn oath to support it. It was not intended that the whole burden of that support should fall on the judicial department. As a matter of fact it rests equally upon every department, although it is in an especial way the concern of the judicial department because it is the duty of the courts to declare and apply the law. In a doubtful case the final responsibility is with the court, but in a case reasonably plain it is the duty of every officer to support it even though his act may have undesirable consequences to himself.[9]

However, as Judge Hand pointed out, legislators—and chief executives, as participants in the legislative process—have the distinctive function of striking net balances and making net adjustments as they confront firsthand facts (often, disputed facts) of community relations and tensions and value choices involved in the factual contexts out of which people bring problems to them. In contrast, most often judges deal with broad standards of constitutional grant or limitation, which normally call on them only to determine whether legislative determinations fall within an outer framework of authorized or permitted legislative action.

Because legislators stand on the front line of making public policy, they are not bound to presume the constitutionality of every bill introduced. To presume so would, indeed, violate their function, which is to make the initial determinations for the legal order of what measures may be in the public interest; this is not a responsibility they may shrug off by a presumption onto the shoulders of proponents of bills; theirs is the task of deciding on net account Yes or No what should go onto the statute books. This was Justice Rosenberry's point for the Wisconsin court.[10] On the other hand, because they are making the initial decisions and are charged with striking a net balance among differing or competing viewpoints and interests for which proponents offer reasonable arguments, legislators normally are not charged to presume against the validity of bills on their docket.[11]

The different degrees of responsibility to constitutional provisions that enter into the legislative function emerge in contrasts between three Presidential interventions in lawmaking by Congress. In *McCulloch v. Maryland* (1819) the Marshall Court upheld the constitutionality of the charter Congress granted to the second Bank of the United States.[12] With a bill before him to extend the Bank's charter for another term, President Jackson asserted his independent responsibility to judge the constitutional authority of Congress to create or extend such an institution, and since—rightly or wrongly—he found the bill to exceed the bounds of Congress's authority, he vetoed it:

> Each public officer who takes an oath to support the Constitution swears that he will support it as he understands it and not as it is understood by others. It is as much the duty of the House of Representatives, of the Senate, and of the President to decide upon the constitutionality of any bill or resolution which may be presented to them for passage or approval as it is of the supreme judges when it may be brought before them for judicial decision. The opinion of the judges has no more authority over Congress than the opinion of Congress has over the judges, and on that point the President is independent of both.[13]

Jackson put in extreme terms the obligation of a policy originator to respect his own oath of fidelity to the Constitution. But he did not announce a general presumption against legislation in any given field; indeed, in the same message he declared his confidence that, if called on, he could propose a bank of the United States that would meet constitutional criteria.[14] Moreover, the force of his pronouncement on his independent responsibility was inherently tempered by the fact that he was refusing to join in a legislative action which the Court had declared allowable; he was not signing a measure which the Court had clearly pronounced to be beyond Congress's authority.

In 1913 Congress passed a bill that became the Webb-Kenyon Act, prohibiting interstate transporation of liquor intended to be held, sold, or used in the original package or otherwise in violation of the law of any state. President Taft vetoed the bill in a message the bulk of which he devoted to his analysis that the bill exceeded Congress's power under the commerce clause as past decisions of the Supreme Court defined that power. He observed that "it is said that this is a question with which the Executive or Members of Congress should not burden themselves to consider or decide. It is said that it should be left to the Supreme Court to say whether this proposed act violates the Constitution." To this proposition Taft dissented "utterly":

> The oath which the Chief Executive takes, and which each member of Congress takes, does not bind him any less sacredly to observe the Constitution than the oaths which the Justices of the Supreme Court take. It is questionable whether the doubtful constitutionality of a bill ought not to furnish a greater reason for voting against the bill, or vetoing it, than for the court to hold it to be invalid. The court will only declare a law invalid where its unconstitutionality is clear, while the lawmaker may very well hesitate to vote for a bill if of doubtful constitutionality because of the wisdom of keeping clearly within the fundamental law. The custom of legislators and executives having any legislative function to remit to the court entire and ultimate responsibility as to the constitutionality of the measures which they take part in passing is an abuse which tends to put the court constantly in opposition to the Legislature and Executive and, indeed, to the popular supporters of unconstitutional laws. If, however, the legislators and the executives had attempted to do their duty this burden of popular disapproval would have been lifted from the courts, or at least considerably lessened.[15]

After considerable debate, Congress passed the bill over the President's veto.[16]

We can bring the policy originator's role into better focus by comparing Taft's veto message with an intervention by President Franklin D. Roosevelt in Congress's consideration of what became the Bituminous Coal Conservation Act of 1935. The bill before Congress undertook certain federal regulations of pricing practices and labor relations in the industry. Lengthy debates, especially in the House of Representatives, centered on the constitutionality of the proposed act. It was in this context that the President addressed an open letter to the chairman of the subcommittee considering the bill. The President asked that the committee recognize that, though bituminous coal deposits lay only in a few states, the coal was consumed nationwide, and that competition and overexpansion had brought destructive price reductions which reacted on labor standards and resulted in disturbance of production and recurring danger of labor conflict. In this setting he indicated his conviction that production conditions in the industry directly affected interstate commerce in coal. With a bow to the Congressional debates on constitutionality, he concluded,

> Manifestly, no one is in a position to give assurance that the proposed act will withstand constitutional tests, for the simple fact that you get not 10 but 1,000 different legal opinions on the subject. But the situation is so urgent and the benefits of the legislation so evident that all doubts should be resolved in favor of the bill, leaving to the courts, in an orderly fashion, the ultimate question of constitutionality. A decision by the Supreme Court relative to this measure, would be helpful as indicating with increasing clarity the constitutional limits within which this Government must operate. The proposed bill has been carefully drafted by employers and employees working cooperatively. An opportunity should be given to the industry to attempt to work out some of its major problems. I hope your committee will not permit doubts as to constitutionality, however reasonable, to block the suggested legislation.[17]

Congress subsequently passed the bill, but in a 6–3 decision the Supreme Court thereafter held that the labor provisions exceeded the commerce power.[18]

President Taft properly demanded that policy originators—legislators and executives participating in the legislative process—accept that their oaths of office bind them to observe constitutional grants and limitations. But he blurred the nature of the constitutional considerations that properly enter into their deliberations. Taft's message did not measure the bill before him in the light of facts of experience and evaluations of that experience, regarding problems that "dry" states had with importation of liquor from "wet" states. Rather he measured the bill against the logic of prior Supreme Court opinions which had expounded the nature of "commerce among the states" in the light of legislation dealing with other subjects.

President Roosevelt poorly phrased his appeal that the Congressional committee "not permit doubts as to constitutionality, however reasonable, to block the suggested legislation." He, too, did not sharply define the "constitutionality" which should concern the legislators. But, in context, his letter did not urge that Congress disregard whether price and labor conditions in the bituminous coal industry might in fact materially burden the conduct of business over state lines; to the contrary, he urged that Congress soberly appraise those matters of fact and soberly evaluate their bearing on the flow of interstate economic dealings. In that aspect he was urging that Congress perform its oath-bound duty to determine whether the proposed federal regulation of the coal industry could reasonably be judged to meet commerce clause criteria. On the other hand, Roosevelt urged that in Congress's appraisal of the economic facts of the industry and their bearing on the conduct of interstate business "all doubts should be resolved in favor of the bill." Thus the President in effect reminded Congress that its responsibility was to make the initial policy determinations, and that inherent in that task was the legitimate function of striking net balances on the elements of fact and value involved. In context, what he particularly asked Congress to subordinate was its judgment as to how far the proposed measure fit within the logic of prior Court-made concepts framed in the light of other issues.

When President Taft claimed that legislators should yield to doubts of "constitutionality", conceived—as he there treated the matter—in terms of prior Court-made doctrine, in effect he disregarded Congress's front-line responsibility to weigh new problems which new circumstances pressed on the primary lawmakers. Some who spoke to override Taft's veto cogently argued that his approach would freeze legislative power into molds set by judges' treatment of past issues, and thus frustrate a prime function of the legislative branch, to deal responsibly with the ongoing, changing experience of the society.[19] The point is underlined by the fact that the Supreme Court later ruled 7–2, that the bill Taft vetoed was within the commerce power. Moreover, though a divided Court in 1936 held the bituminous coal act in part invalid, in 1937 a divided Court in substance overruled the doctrine followed in 1936.[20] The net wisdom to draw from such events is that oaths to observe constitutional grants and limitations create different obligations for those whose function is to originate public policy and for those whose function is to review determinations of policy.

The Range of Findings and Choices Implicit in a Statute. Implicit (though not always explicitly declared) in a legislature's decision to enact a statute are four types of determinations. In most instances courts in the late twentieth century recognize that as reviewing bodies they should defer to the judgment of the policy originators regarding all four. To understand the reach and operation of the presumption of constitutionality which judges apply to most statutes we need to identify these four kinds of legislative judgments.

A statute typically embodies the legislature's choice of some goal to be achieved for the benefit of what the legislators see or claim as the general interest (i.e., what ought to be done for the sake of some objective the legislature deems of public interest). Also, a statute typically embodies the legislature's choice of some means for reaching the goal (i.e., what ought to be done as a means of achieving the desired objective). Philosophers may find such a distinction between ends and means a crude, if not often a question-begging device for analyzing human experience. But the distinction sufficiently corresponds to the usual matter-of-fact approach of lawmakers to their job to serve our purposes in analyzing legal administration. Under each of these heads of ends and means, in passing a statute the legislature normally makes two other determinations insofar as it operates with some workable minimum of rationality. It finds the existence of some facts of human behavior or of physical or biological reality bearing on human experience (i.e., it finds what is—what facts exist—relevant to making judgments about choices of ends and means). Such facts may be in themselves value-neutral; that individuals or firms buy and sell Commodity X does not in itself tell us that it is either good or bad that they do so, only that they do so. But passing a statute is an act of choice, expressing needs or wants and some rank ordering of needs and wants; in addition to such findings of fact as it explicitly or implicitly embodies, a statute which bans the sale of Commodity X constitutes a value choice, expressing a politically effective opinion that such dealings are bad for people, or at least should be subordinated to some other needs or wants that people experience. Thus a statute normally involves four basic elements: choices of Ends and Means, and determinations of What Is and of What Ought to be Done about what is. This is the pattern:

Statute

End: What Ought to be Done
What is

Means: What Ought to be Done
What Is

Judicial opinions do not regularly spell out all these elements; the opinion by Judge Learned Hand from which I earlier quoted is exceptionally explicit, particularly in emphasizing the presence in the statute of both legislative findings of fact and legislative choice of values.[21] But the elements are there in most cases, to be found if one cultivates some skill in reading between the lines. Consider the Supreme Court's opinion in *Powell v. Pennsylvania* (1888).[22] It is a rather old case. Involving a due process challenge to a statute penalizing sale of oleomargarine, it has an obsolete cast in our view.[23] But the pattern of analysis the Court there developed stands validated by late twentieth-century decisions on the presumption of constitutionality applied to legislation regulating the marketplace.[24]

Quoting Chief Justice Waite, in an earlier case, that "every possible presumption is in favor of the validity of a statute," the

Court first applied the presumption on the issue of the validity of the statute's declared purposes, to protect public health and prevent fraud. The Court ruled that, on the record in the suit before it,

> it cannot adjudge that the defendant's rights of liberty and property . . . have been infringed by the statute of Pennsylvania, without holding that, although it may have been enacted in good faith for the objects expressed in its title . . . it has, in fact, no real or substantial relation to those objects.[25]

But the Court recognized that the challenge ran to the means as well as to the ends of the statute. The act wholly banned sale of the product, rather than providing procedures to distinguish between properly or improperly produced goods. The Court applied the presumption of constitutionality also to this issue of the reasonableness of the means adopted:

> Whether the manufacture of oleomargarine . . . is, or may be, conducted in such a way or with such skill and secrecy as to baffle ordinary inspection, or whether it involves such danger to the public health as to require, for the protection of the people, the entire suppression of the business, rather than its regulation in such manner as to permit the manufacture and sale of articles of that class that do not contain noxious ingredients, are questions of fact and of public policy which belong to the legislative department to determine.

Within the issues both of the validity of the ends and that of the means adopted by the statute, the Court recognized the presence of challenges to the legislature's judgments on the fact basis and on the value choice embodied in the legislation. On the question whether the regulation might be deemed related to the end of protecting public health, the Court found the challenger's offer of proof of the safety of his product to be insufficient, because it did not deal with the full range of facts with which the legislature might be concerned:

> It is entirely consistent with [defendant's] . . . offer [of proof] that many, indeed, most kinds of oleomargarine butter in the market contain ingredients that are or may become injurious to health.

> The court cannot say, from anything of which it may take judicial cognizance, that such is not the fact.

Similarly, on the reasonableness of the means adopted—total suppression of the trade—the Court observed that at stake were "questions of fact and of public policy which belong to the legislative department to determine." Whether the focus be on the existence of a reasonable basis for the legislature's determination of facts relevant to its enactment or on the reasonableness of the value choices it made, the Court must hold itself to its reviewer's role:

> It is not a part of . . . [the courts'] functions to conduct investigations of facts entering into questions of public policy merely, and to sustain or frustrate the legislative will, embodied in statutes, as they may happen to approve or to disapprove its determination of such questions. The power which the legislature has to promote the general welfare is very great, and the discretion which that department of the government has, in the employment of means to that end, is very large.[26]

Constitutional Standards and Constitutional Rules. Constitutions contain two types of provisions, distinguished by the generality or particularity of their terms. The distinction is especially marked in the United States Constitution. Some grants or limitations declare standards—declarations of values and of circumstances that evoke them, cast in broad categories which can include a considerable range of particular applications. A peculiarly important grant clause framed as a standard is that which authorizes Congress "to regulate commerce . . . among the several states." Treated by the Supreme Court as carrying implicit curbs on nondiscriminatory state legislation that unduly burdens conduct of interstate trade, the commerce clause stands also as a constitutional limitation that the Court has developed as a standard. The due process clauses of the Fifth and Fourteenth Amendments, taken by the Supreme Court to set judicially defined limits on the substance of legislative power, are also limitations that have the breadth of standards. It inheres in constitutional standards that their application requires fresh inquiry into the fact and value context of each assertion of legislative authority and of each challenged exercise of legislative authority. That Congress may regulate prices charged for interstate air carriage under the commerce clause does not settle that it may regulate wages and hours of broad classes of workers engaged in interstate and local trade. That on some terms, without running afoul of substantive due process, a state may regulate use of saccharin in foodstuffs does not settle that there is no due process barrier to regulating use of red dye in foodstuffs. Under the strong presumption of constitutionality applied to most economic regulatory legislation in the late twentieth century, judges uphold most such statutes, but they do so in light of the particular fact and value context of each policy subject.[27]

Constitutions also contain rules—provisions detailing government structures or procedures, or declaring in specific terms certain values and the circumstances in which the values come into play. Speaking for the Court, Chief Justice Hughes distinguished such constitutional rules from constitutional standards:

> When the provisions of the Constitution, in grant or restriction, are specific, so particularized as not to admit of construction, no question is presented. Thus, emergency would not permit a State to have more than two Senators in the Congress, or permit the election of President by a general popular vote without regard to the number of electors to which the States are respectively entitled, or permit the States to "coin money" or to "make anything but gold and silver a tender in payment of debts." But where constitutional grants and limitations of power are set forth in general clauses, which afford a broad outline, the process of construction is essential to fill in the details.[28]

Most constitutional provisions that come into litigation over the validity of statutes are standards. Their breadth of reach into affairs carries two characteristics relevant to defining the role of judges as reviewers rather than originators of policy. Measuring a statute against a constitutional standard usually calls for invoking knowledge of matters that lie outside the expertise of law-trained individuals and outside the domain of legal treatises.

worthless. For the Court, Chief Justice Hughes declared that

> Not only are existing laws read into contracts in order to fix obligations as between the parties, but the reservation of essential attributes of sovereign power is also read into contracts as a postulate of the legal order. The policy of protecting contracts against impairment presupposes the maintenance of a government by virtue of which contractual relations are worth while—a government which retains adequate authority to secure the peace and good order of society. . . . The economic interests of the State may justify the exercise of its continuing and dominant protective power notwithstanding interference with contracts. . . . The question is . . . whether the legislation is addressed to a legitimate end and the measures taken are reasonable and appropriate to that end.[36]

However, on its face the contract clause indicates that the Constitution puts a preferred value on protecting prior commitments of economic assets against disturbance by retroactive state laws. In this light one should not expect clear application of the presumption of constitutionality in this area. I have noted that the Court does not bring the presumption into play where issues are drawn in terms of defining protected "contracts" and forbidden "impairment". Though *Blaisdell* treated the protected "obligation" of contracts as involving a constitutional standard rather than a rule, the Court's opinion upheld the Minnesota moratorium statute on the basis of the positive case made for it by its supporters; the temper of the opinion is not that of the ordinary presumption of constitutionality. Moreover, in other cases where the Court deemed the purpose of challenged legislation—measured by its terms or by its predictable effect—to be directly to change the allocation of benefits or costs of a bargain as the parties had set these by their prior agreement, even though the legislation might serve some other, non-market public interest, the Court has not treated the issue as if it were to be resolved under a presumption in favor of the statute.[37]

The original meaning of the due process clauses of the Fifth and Fourteenth Amendments was to set a criterion for legal procedures.[38] The Supreme Court's decisions indicate that we

These are in part What Is questions implicit in legislative action, which cannot be answered simply from what lawyers know about the world. When the Pennsylvania legislature banned sale of oleomargarine for the declared purpose of protecting public health, the challenge raised under the due process clause required judges to appraise whether facts known to experts in chemistry, nutrition, or medicine gave reasonable basis for legislators to believe that oleomargarine might make people sick. The due process challenge also posed problems of weighing competing values—issues of What Ought We To Do about the facts. The judges must decide whether the legislature could reasonably determine that the degree of danger to health warranted subordinating the social value generally attached to operations of the private market, free of legal intervention. Such fact-enmeshed value choices are another kind which cannot be answered simply from knowledge contained in law books.[29]

The particularity of constitutional rules has its own character which warrants a different role for judges in reviewing the validity of legislation challenged under such criteria. Application of constitutional rules usually does not require that judges resort to knowledge of matters outside of official texts and law books. Typically application of a constitutional rule turns either on facts readily determined through familiar processes of interpreting formal language of the law (as in deciding that the President may not be elected directly by popular vote), or on facts wholly defined out of legal learning. Of the latter type is the question posed by applying the clauses of the national Constitution which forbid Congress or the states to pass an "ex post facto law."[30] The meaning of the term *ex post facto law* is a meaning created by judges and lawyers in administering legal order, and given further definition in legal treatises. To apply the constitutional rule, judges need draw only on their knowledge of legal doctrine and legal history and apply familiar legal skills in interpreting statutes. If from such wholly legal skill and learning they find that the statute before them makes unlawful and subjects to criminal penalty or to extremely burdensome civil obligations or disabilities conduct that the affected person engaged in before the law was passed and that was lawful conduct when the person acted, they thereupon know all the facts they need to know to apply the clause. Further, the specificity of such a constitutional rule leaves legislators no room for weighing and choosing among competing values. By their sharply focused language the constitution makers have made the value choice: No "law and order" crisis felt by the legislature will warrant it in passing an ex post facto law. Where a constitutional rule applies, its particularity frees judges of obligation to defer to legislative judgment either on What Is issues or on issues of What We Ought To Do about the relevant facts.[31]

However, the matter is not quite that simple. Judges enjoy a larger measure of power vis-à-vis the legislature only within the area of policy they deem governed by rule. Decisions show that the Supreme Court treats some constitutional problems as combining standard and rule elements. Though the cases are not wholly consistent or the doctrine plainly defined, the ban on ex post facto laws has generally supported rather summary upset of laws retroactively imposing what the Court finds to fall within familiar categories of criminal penalties.[32] On the other hand, where statutes of retroactive operation impose civil burdens or disabilities—such as disqualifying from certain professions individuals previously convicted of felonies—to accomplish what the judges estimate to be primarily prospective regulation of civil affairs, the Court has found that the ex post facto clause does not apply. Thus the Court has held that the ex post facto clause does not bar a statute which disqualifies from practice of medicine individuals previously convicted of felonies; instead, applying the ordinary presumption of constitutionality, it has asked only whether legislators could reasonably decide that protection of public health required legal safeguard of patients against putting themselves in the hands of practitioners whose past behavior indicated them to be of unsavory character.[33]

An analogous distinction appears in cases under the clause of the United States Constitution which declares that "No state shall . . . pass any . . . law impairing the obligation of contracts."[34] The opinions in which the Marshall Court decided

that the contract clause protected deeds of land and charters of incorporation against retroactive legislation contained no words of deference owed to legislative fact findings or value judgments. Plainly, in deciding what were "contracts" and what kinds of retroactive statutory provisions would "impair" the obligation of contracts, the Court felt confident that its own legal learning, applied to the language of the constitutional rule and of the challenged legislation, fully equipped it to resolve the issues, combining with the judgment of the constitution makers its own judgment of the nature of the protection they meant to give.[35]

In contrast, the Court has treated as a constitutional standard that aspect of the contract clause which forbids impairing the "obligation" of contracts. Not every private agreement receives protection and enforcement from government; the society reserves to itself authority to determine what private agreements are consistent with a healthy state of social relationships, and which tend to produce such antisocial consequences that the state should refuse to enforce them or should even punish those who make them. To determine that a private agreement is against the good order of society may involve appraising questions of fact to which legal learning does not give answers, and weighing competing fact-enmeshed values on which law-trained individuals as such are not experts. Such a situation calls on judges to practice deference toward legislative judgments. In *Home Building & Loan Association v. Blaisdell* (1934) the Supreme Court confronted a Minnesota statute creating a limited moratorium on foreclosure and sale under defaulted mortgages. A down-spiraling economy had produced a surge of mortgage foreclosures; as more and more land was thrown into the market on foreclosure sales, land values plummeted; in turn this course of events imperilled the financial integrity of the general economy of the state, and especially of its banks and insurance companies. In this setting the Supreme Court treated the contract clause protection of the "obligation" of mortgage contracts as allowing reasonable discretion to the state legislature to determine when routine enforcement of ordinary remedies might bring down the whole economy and thus render all contracts

must be somewhat cautious in treating the requirements of procedural due process as setting a constitutional rule or a constitutional standard. Where a statute sets out certain procedures for enforcing legal rights or duties in situations long familiar to the law, within long-sustained judicial tradition and experience of certain modes of enforcement, the Court will probably treat procedural due process as a matter of fixed, particular rule, and give short shrift to a drastic legislative departure from the established pattern. Here the judges are likely to feel that they are on factual grounds fully familiar to them out of their knowledge and experience as law-trained individuals, and that the values at stake have definition and weight also fully derived from legal knowledge and experience. So it is not surprising that we find no reference to a presumption of constitutionality—and a decision reached wholly in terms of judge-made concepts of what procedural due process requires—in *Pennoyer v. Neff* (1877), requiring service of process on an individual within the sovereign's territory as a basis for a judgment in personam for money.[39] But where a statute set procedures of a novel sort in new areas of policy, the Court followed the presumption of constitutionality. Upholding a statutory procedure for terminating foster parent relations, the Court emphasized that the legislature was breaking new ground: "We deal here with issues of unusual delicacy, in an area where professional judgments regarding desirable procedures are constantly and rapidly changing. In such a context, restraint is appropriate on the part of courts, called upon to adjudicate whether a particular procedural scheme is adequate under the Constitution."[40]

THE PRESUMPTION OF CONSTITUTIONALITY

Early sensitive to the elements distinctive to the institutional relations between the legislative and judicial processes, the Supreme Court emphasized that it should take peculiar care in dealing with challenges to the constitutionality of a statute. For the Court Chief Justice Marshall cautioned in 1810 that:

> The question, whether a law be void for its repugnancy to the

> constitution, is, at all times, a question of much delicacy, which ought seldom, if ever, to be decided in the affirmative in a doubtful case. The court, when impelled by duty to render such a judgment, would be unworthy of its station, could it be unmindful of the solemn obligations which that station imposes. But it is not on slight implication and vague conjectures that the legislature is to be pronounced to have transcended its powers, and its acts to be considered as void. The opposition between the constitution and the law should be such that the judges feel a clear and strong conviction of their incompatability with each other.[41]

Translated into terms of courtroom combat, Marshall's approach means that one challenging the constitutionality of a statute normally must bear a heavy burden of sustaining the claim.

The Burden of Persuasion. The position thus taken by the Court has found standard expression in the formula which declares that normally we should presume that a statute is constitutional until a challenger plainly shows the contrary.[42] Where application of a constitutional standard such as substantive due process requires judges to consider matters of fact underlying the legislative judgment which lie outside the domain of legal learning and to appraise a legislative choice of fact-enmeshed values on which legal learning supplies no ready calculus, some allocation of the burden of persuasion among contending parties serves a useful purpose of legal administration. In such a situation the judges need to be informed on matters that lie outside their legal training. An allocation of the burden of persuasion assists the court by putting pressure on counsel to bring needed information before the judges. Conceivably, however, the court might put the burden always on the supporter of the legislation. That it normally puts the burden on the challenger shows that some consideration other than a merely utilitarian value underlies the presumption of constitutionality. The deeper value is regard for the separation of powers. The supporter comes into court with the advantage that another responsible legal agency, the legislature, has already examined the questions of fact and value choice embodied in the statute. As Learned Hand pointed out, regard for the constitutional division of labor means that the judges should not presume to do afresh what the legislators have already done; proper deference to the legislature's role puts on the challenger the burden of persuasion that the act violates a constitutional standard.[43]

These utility and separation of powers values do not apply where colorable claim is made that the statute offends a constitutional rule. A constitutional rule usually presents no questions of fact outside the competence of law-trained individuals, and embodies a value choice made by the constitution makers which leaves no discretion of choice to the legislature. Thus if a statute on its face has the character of an ex post facto law we should not expect to find that the court places the burden of persuasion on the challenger, but rather that it requires the supporter to show reason why the ex post facto clause does not apply.[44]

Against the background of the various factors I have now considered we can better appreciate the character of the presumption of constitutionality. At first encounter one may be inclined to regard that formula as a rhetorical flourish. But closer examination shows that the presumption is a somewhat complex structure which provides a useful pattern for analyzing, arguing, and deciding constitutional issues. In practice judges have not always adhered to it even when they have continued to acknowledge it. But at least since the mid–1930s the Supreme Court has given it strong application affecting the bulk of legislation. And in any event it offers lawyers a useful instrument for giving analytical order to most of their jousting on issues of the validity of statutes. Whether we regard the presumption as a serviceable guide in predicting what judges may do, or only as a useful tool of lawyers' argument, one conclusion emerges plainly from detailed examination of its elements. Where it applies, the presumption provides a great bulwark to the supporter of a statute, and a high hurdle to the challenger.

Base and Reach of the Presumption of Constitutionality. The supporter of a statute must show that a proper base exists for invoking the presumption. However, his task is a simple one. In areas of policy where the presumption applies, he brings the presumption into play merely by showing that the statute is on the books and that the constitutional issue arises under a constitutional standard and not under a constitutional rule. From the fact that the legislature passed the act, the court will presume that the legislators had reasonable grounds for finding the existence of facts relevant to their policy judgment and for making the choice of values they made. That the existence of the statute suffices as the base of the presumption appears most sharply where the court upholds the legislation in a lawsuit in which the supporter has made no effective case on behalf of the act other than citing it. Such an example was *Powell v. Pennsylvania.* The state indicted Powell for a sale of oleomargarine contrary to the statutory ban. The case was tried on a stipulation of facts, that on a given date in the city of Harrisburg the defendant sold to the prosecuting witness as an article of food two original packages of oleomargarine, and that he then had in his possession 100 pounds of oleomargarine with intent to sell it as an article of food. "This", the Court observed, "was the case made by the Commonwealth." The defendant offered some expert testimony on the safe quality of his oleomargarine, which the Court ruled to be irrelevant and immaterial. The Court sustained the validity of the act. Thus the state won its case on a record which contained nothing on behalf of the statute except that it stood on Pennsylvania's statute books; the matters set out in the stipulation of facts did not relate to the validity of the statute, but only showed that the defendant had engaged in conduct that violated the terms of the act.[45] That the existence of the statute is enough to raise the presumption is also implicit in decisions that there is no requirement that the statute on its face declare its rationale, or that there be a legislative record or formal findings in support of the act.[46]

Given that the base of the presumption calls only for showing the existence of the statute and that the challenger presents an issue raised under a constitutional standard, the presumption of constitutionality, especially as applied in the later half of the twentieth century, normally operates over a wide range of questions. It applies where the issue is of the scope of broad grants of power to legislatures, as under the United States Constitution's authorizations to Congress to tax and spend and to regulate commerce among the states.[47] It applies to the broad limitations on national and state legislative power that courts find in the substantive aspects of due process and equal protection clauses.[48] It applies to the limits that the Supreme Court has found implicit in the commerce clause on nondiscriminatory state legislation unduly burdening interstate commerce.[49] In their practice of generously upholding legislative grants of rule-making power to executive and administrative agencies, courts in effect apply the presumption on behalf of delegations of power, though they do not usually make the point explicit.[50] Beyond these categories, decisions apply the presumption to such a miscellany of other issues of legislative authority that we can fairly say that the norm is to treat the presumption as a residual guide to judicial review, in play wherever a constitutional rule is not in issue and wherever judges do not find some special basis for exercising more strict scrutiny.[51]

Weight of the Burden of Persuasion Put on Challenger. Speaking for the Court in *Powell v. Pennsylvania*, Justice Harlan quoted Chief Justice Waite, that "Every possible presumption is in favor of the validity of a statute, and this continues until the contrary is shown beyond a rational doubt."[52] In analogy to the burden of proof placed on the government to convict an accused of a crime, this formula put on one who challenged the constitutionality of a statute the most severe burden of persuasion known to our law. The Supreme Court has continued to invoke this charge or to declare its equivalent by requiring that the challenger show that the legislative determinations in question are "arbitrary", that is, incapable of reasoned justification.[53] A practical consequence is that if—from material presented by the statute's supporter or provided by judicial notice or appearing from the challenger's own presentation—some material conflict of evidence appears regarding the legislature's fact findings or choice of values, the conflict itself shows that the court should uphold the statute, if the issue is in an area governed by the presumption of constitutionality.[54]

The weight of the burden put on the challenger precludes simple formulas for rebutting the presumption of constitutionality. Thus evidence sufficient to establish a litigant's standing to raise an issue of constitutionality does not in itself suffice to rebut the presumption. In *Powell v. Pennsylvania* the Court sustained the state's objection that Powell's evidence of losses he would suffer on investments made in machinery and inventory before the act was passed was "immaterial and irrelevant" to the issue he raised of violation of substantive due process. Powell of course had standing to raise the constitutional issue simply because the state had made him defendant in a criminal prosecution. However, his attack on the statute gained no force from the circumstances of economic loss, which would have given him standing to bring a bill to enjoin enforcement of the act.[55] The issue was drawn sharply in *Hegeman Farms Corporation v. Baldwin* (1934).[56] The plaintiff, a wholesale milk dealer, sued to enjoin enforcement against him of orders of the New York Milk Control Board under legislation regulating prices in the industry. The bill alleged that, within the prices the regulatory pattern allowed plaintiff to charge, he was unable to earn a fair return on the present fair value of his investment less depreciation. The allegation may have sufficed to show standing. But on the merits the trial court granted the defendant's motion to dismiss the bill, and the Supreme Court affirmed. For the Court Justice Cardozo explained,

> The bill and findings . . . do not tell us whether the appellant ran its business with reasonable efficiency when compared with others in its calling. They do not even tell us whether it was earning a fair return on its investment before the orders were adopted. . . . The appellant's grievance amounts to this, that it is operating at a loss, though other dealers more efficient or economical or better known to the public may be operating at a profit. A bill of com-

> plaint so uncertain in aim and so meagre in particulars falls short of the standard of candor and precision set up by our decisions. . . . If the designation of a minimum price is within the scope of the police power, expenses or losses made necessary thereby must be borne as an incident, unless the order goes so far beyond the needs of the occasion as to be turned into an act of tyranny. Nothing of the sort is charged. The Fourteenth Amendment does not protect a business against the hazards of competition.[57]

Other formulas of like simplicity fail to rebut the presumption of constitutionality, given the severe burden it casts on the challenger of a statute. That a statute creating civil regulations operates retroactively does not in itself constitute a rebuttal.[58] That a statute drastically changes prior common law doctrine, however familiar and long-standing, does not of itself upset the presumption. Thus, for the Court Justice Holmes ruled tersely that whether by statute a state may regulate entry into the banking business "is not answered by citing authorities for the existence of the right at common law. There are many things that a man might do at common law that the States may forbid."[59] Nor is the presumption rebutted by showing that a regulatory act may confer special profit or advantage upon a private interest, so long as it appears that the legislature could reasonably find that the statute may also serve a public interest; concurrence of public and private gain from legislation is so common in a society of diverse and interweaving interests that judges would substantially abrogate the legislative function if they held that such parallelism alone made a statute unconstitutional.[60]

The Scope of Required Rebuttal of the Presumption of Constitutionality. In *Powell v. Pennsylvania* the challenger offered expert testimony that the oleomargarine he produced was healthy. This evidence aimed directly at the statute's declared purpose of protecting public health. But the Court ruled that it was irrelevant, for it was "entirely consistent with that offer [of proof] that many, indeed, that most kinds of oleomargarine butter in the market contain ingredients that are or may become injurious to health."[61] The defendant's evidence might rebut a justification for the statute based on the proposition that all oleomargarine was dangerous. But it did nothing to rebut the other possible justification which the Court noted. Thus if there are two or three reasonable hypotheses to support the validity of a statute, the presumption of constitutionality requires that the challenger rebut all of them, or lose his case. The Court has applied this exacting test in other cases, though one can find instances in which judges ask less of a challenger.[62] In any event the rebuttal formula of *Powell v. Pennsylvania* is important for the swordplay of contending counsel—potentially of high argumentative utility to a lawyer who relies on a statute, of high embarrassment to one who attacks a statute. However, judges use common sense. Justice Harlan's opinion for the Court in *Powell* notes that the presumption calls on the judges only to hypothesize "reasonable grounds" for the statute.[63] The challenger does not have to rebut every notion that ingenious imagination might contrive to justify the legislation.[64]

The litigant who relies on a statute need not prove that the legislature in fact had in mind such reasonable justifications as he suggests would warrant the act; he is entitled to ground the presumption of constitutionality simply on the fact that the statute stands on the books. "For these purposes [of the presumption]," the Court has said, "it is, of course constitutionally irrelevant whether this reasoning in fact underlay the legislative decision, as it is irrelevant that the challenged [statutory] section does not apply to all to whom the postulated rationale might in logic apply."[65] However, the situation may perhaps be altered if, as is not uncommon, the legislature has included in its statute a preamble explicitly stating a particular rationale. One may fairly question whether, if the challenger rebuts the declared rationale, he should be required to go further and offer rebuttal to other conceivable bases for the act which the legislature did not choose to mention. The Supreme Court has not spoken plainly to this point, but some opinions indicate that the Court may require of the challenger that he rebut only the justification which the statutory text explicitly sets out.[66] There is a caution here for draftsmen. The legislature does not violate the separation of powers by declaring its findings and justification in a preamble, and such a declaration, though not binding on the judges, may add substantial support to the presumption of constitutionality.[67] But the presence of the preamble may also deny the statute the full range of supporting hypotheses which the court might be willing to invoke where the legislature has not committed itself to a specified rationale.

Influence of the State of the Record Made in Litigation. Where a litigant challenges the validity of a statute by reference to a constitutional standard that presents issues of fact or of fact-enmeshed values which judges cannot resolve simply out of legal learning, the state of the record made in the lawsuit may be critical to the outcome. In the second half of the twentieth century judges' practice teaches that lawyers should not assume that they can safely try a constitutional issue in the same way in which they might try a suit for breach of contract or for personal injury. A prime difference centers on use of procedures—demurrers or motions of equivalent effect—designed to segregate an issue of law for decision simply on the parties' pleadings.

The cases indicate disfavor toward any litigant—supporter or challenger—who in this situation seeks to obtain a decision simply on the pleadings; increasingly sensitive to the limits of their knowledge where constitutional questions take them outside familiar domains of law books, judges tend to press for creation of a full record based on documentary or witness-stand testimony as to the fact and value premises of the challenged legislation. Thus where the challenger moved to strike the supporter's pleading relying on a New Jersey statute regulating insurance agents' commissions, incident to regulating insurance rates, for the Court Justice Brandeis invoked the full strength of the presumption of constitutionality to uphold the statute:

> The statute here questioned deals with a subject clearly within the scope of the police power. We are asked to declare it void on the ground that the specific method of regulation prescribed is unreasonable and hence deprives the plaintiff of due process of

> law. As underlying questions of fact may condition the constitutionality of legislation of this character, the presumption of constitutionality must prevail in the absence of some factual foundation of record for overthrowing the statute. It does not appear upon the face of the statute, or from any facts of which the court must take judicial notice, that in New Jersey evils did not exist in the business of fire insurance for which this statutory provision was an appropriate remedy. The action of the Legislature and of the highest court of the State indicates that such evils did exist. The record is barren of any allegation of fact tending to show unreasonableness.[68]

On the other hand, when the challenger of a New York statutory regulation on milk prices sued to enjoin enforcement of the regulation as denying equal protection of law and the supporter moved to dismiss the plaintiff's bill, the Court refused to decide the case on the merits at that stage. Instead, the Court remanded for a trial on evidence which might show what the legislature might reasonably have found as to economic conditions in the New York City milk market and what reasonable assessment they might have made of the competing social values at stake. In the Court's judgment the allegations in the plaintiff's bill for an injunction, supplemented by the Court's judicial notice that plaintiff's business conduct fell within what had theretofore been commonly regarded as socially acceptable business practice, made out a prima facie case against the regulation. Evidently the Court felt that in that posture the supporter of the challenged regulation was seeking an unfair advantage by invoking the presumption of constitutionality and also by the motion to dismiss which, if granted, would bar the challenger from any opportunity to present a record of evidence to bulwark his attack.[69]

As Justice Brandeis indicated in his observations in the New Jersey case, it is not impossible that judges might feel themselves sufficiently equipped to decide a constitutional challenge presented on the pleadings, though the issue takes them outside the domain of legal learning. But the decisions call for special caution where the lawsuit puts in question the validity of a statute. For the purposes of decision on a demurrer a court will assume to be true well-pleaded allegations of fact set out in the pleading to which a litigant demurs. Thus if a challenger's allegations provide a comprehensive essay on the community situation with reference to which the legislature acted, they may provide a basis on which the court can feel entitled to decide the merits of the constitutional issue. However, in a complex policy situation even a talented pleader is likely to have great difficulty in setting out with concrete particularity the context of facts and values relevant to appraising the legislation. Hence we should expect judges to be wary of finding enough simply in a pleader's recitations to ground a decision against the validity of a statute. So with some strictness the Supreme Court has ordinarily insisted that "the burden [of the challenger] is not sustained by making allegations which are merely the general conclusions of law or fact. . . . Facts relied upon to rebut the presumption of constitutionality must be specifically set forth. . . . A motion to dismiss like a demurrer, admits only facts well pleaded."[70]

Another way in which matters of fact underlying the constitutionality of a statute may be established, apart from witness-stand testimony or documentary evidence, is by judicial notice, whether the case is heard on pleadings only or on a record made at trial. However, the test for judicial notice is a stringent one—that the fact be known beyond reasonable dispute by those knowledgeable in the relevant field of experience, whether the field calls for specialist or expert knowledge or for knowledge people gain from everyday experience. Given the gravity of the issue where the validity of a statute is at stake, judges should scrupulously observe the limits of resort to judicial notice. But this is an aspect of the handling of constitutional issues often marked by naive, loose, or apparently prejudiced handling. Judicial opinions often rely on assertions of fact for which there is no record evidence, without acknowledging that they are in effect drawing on judicial notice and measuring their reliance against the severe criterion the law sets. A prime responsibility of a lawyer on behalf of his client in a contest over the validity of a statute may be to keep alert to identify such unacknowledged resort to judicial notice by opposing counsel or by a judge, and insist on measuring the propriety of such use.[71] We should be careful, too, to observe the limits of resort to judicial notice as bearing on the constitutional question, even where judicial notice is otherwise appropriate. Judicial notice may supply matter that supports the validity of a statute.[72] But this does not mean that absence of material that may be judicially noticed to uphold the act will be fatal to its validity. If counsel and court are sensitive to the requirements of the presumption of constitutionality, they will put the matter in the negative; if no other showing is made, the court should presume the statute constitutional from the fact of its enactment, unless a rebuttal is made out by judicial notice or by record evidence.[73]

The Practicability of Meeting the Burden of Persuasion on Issues of the Constitutionality of Statutes. Where a litigant questions the validity of a statute measured against a constitutional standard involving issues of fact and values the answers to which do not lie simply in legal learning, a skeptic may ask whether prevailing doctrine in reality allows practical possibility of rebutting the presumption of constitutionality. Where the presumption applies, the Supreme Court in the later twentieth century declares it with a strength which may seem in effect to preclude rebuttal. Especially where the challenged legislation regulates conduct in the private marketplace, the working impact of the "presumption" may seem to amount to a rule of law that the Court simply will not hold such a statute invalid on due process or equal protection grounds.[74] In areas of preferred values, where the Court puts on the supporter of a challenged act a comparably severe burden of persuasion, an analogous question might be raised.

However, both in the ordinary case and in relation to preferred-value areas, the Supreme Court's formulas normally continue to leave the door ajar for either rebuttal of the presumption by a challenger or persuasion of the validity of a suspect act by a supporter.[75] Moreover, most lawsuits over the validity of statutes end in state and federal trial courts or in federal courts of appeal or in state appellate courts. Especially in state courts the Reports show more variation in treatment of such issues than appears in the Supreme Court of the United States; state Reports in particular show a fair number of appellate decisions which find that the challenger has rebutted the presumption of constitutionality.[76] Hence lawyers need to be equipped to deal with the presumption of constitutionality or the formulas applied in preferred-value areas, because they cannot safely assume that all judges will closely observe the limitations which the Supreme Court sets on judicial review. Furthermore, state constitutions contain limitations analogous to the due process and equal protection clauses of the national Constitution, and these—as well as other grants or limitations peculiar to state constitutions—provide non-federal bases on which state courts have the final word as they entertain challenges to the validity of state legislation. Generally state courts follow the Supreme Court's lead in setting norms for the trial of constitutional issues. But they are not bound to do so.[77] This independence of state judges is another reason why lawyers should understand the strategic and tactical guides for constitutional argument provided by the Supreme Court's development of the presumption of constitutionality and its opposite.

Areas of Constitutionally Preferred Values. In the second half of the twentieth century the Supreme Court has begun elaborating categories of what it has deemed constitutionally preferred values, in the face of which it has not applied the presumption of constitutionality to a challenged statute. Instead, in such areas of policy in somewhat varying degree the Court has put on the supporter some burden of making a positive case on behalf of the act. By the 1980s, apart from issues under the contract clause, five principal categories of preferred values had emerged, which in descending order progress from quite specific to quite indefinite boundaries. These categories in which the supporter must meet some substantial burden of persuasion to uphold the legislation concern (1) statutes which make race (or, probably, ethnic or religious origin) a criterion for determining rights, duties or privileges under law to the detriment of an historically disadvantaged group; (2) state statutes that appear explicitly or in demonstrated practical impact to discriminate against interstate commerce; (3) statutes that hinder or tend to suppress rational processes in the making of public policy, by limiting the right to vote, creating congressional districts of unequal numbers of voters, or burdening freedom of speech, assembly, or press in matters of public policymaking; (4) statutes that burden processes of public communication outside the domain of public affairs, through the arts, or through the press as this bears on other than political matters; and (5) statutes the Court deems to deny the intrinsic worth or dignity of individuals by intruding on areas of life which people value as private and not of public concern, involving freedom of religion, the internal affairs of the family, childbearing, and private pursuit of sex experience.[78]

It took from John Marshall's day (1810) to *Powell v. Pennsylvania* (1888) to Judge Learned Hand's analysis in 1935 to develop a fairly full pattern of what the presumption of constitutionality means to the contending moves of lawyers and the analysis of judges in dealing with the validity of a statute.[79] Since preferred-values analysis took on salience only from the late 1930s, it is not surprising that by the 1980s the Supreme Court has not yet spelled out in consistent detail what that analysis means for the moves and countermoves of lawyers and the criteria for judicial dispositions. However, when the Court designates an issue as falling within a preferred value category, it plainly means to prescribe a different treatment of the matter than would obtain under the ordinary presumption of constitutionality.

The challenger lays a base for placing the burden of justifying a statute on its supporter if the challenger shows that by its explicit terms the act trespasses on a constitutionally preferred value or uses means inconsistent with that value. Thus in *McLaughlin v. Florida* (1964) the Court held invalid a state statute imposing a criminal penalty for cohabitation by a black and a white; on this showing the Court ruled that the state had a heavy burden of justifying the regulation, and had not met its burden.[80] The situation is not so clear where the statute on its face does not infringe a preferred value, but the challenger claims that its working effect is to do so. If the challenger convinces the court that the only reasonably predictable effect of the statute will be to invade the constitutionally preferred value, he will have done enough to rebut the regular presumption of constitutionality, if that be applicable, or at least to shift to the supporter a heavy burden of justification.[81] If the statute may fairly be deemed to serve some valid public end, but the challenger offers persuasive evidence that in operation it will also have a disproportionately adverse impact on a specially favored constitutional value, the challenger may put on the supporter the burden of making a strong case that a legitimate goal may be served; if the supporter can meet that criterion, then the Court apparently will reject the attack unless the challenger can prove actual intent in the legislative body to invade the specially protected value.[82] The decisions do not require the supporter to show more than one justifying ground for the statute; proper regard for the legislature's legitimate function does not call for more.[83]

When the challenger has established a base for a preferred-value attack on a statute, the Court has fixed two levels of burden of justification to be laid on the supporter of the act. Some preferred constitutional values, it appears, claim more deference than others. At the highest level stand constitutional bans on invidious use of racial criteria in law and on interference with free speech and kindred activities of communication involved in public policymaking. Where the statute "trenches upon the constitutionally protected freedom from invidious official discrimination based on race," the legislation "even though enacted pursuant to a valid state interest, bears a heavy burden of justification. . . . and will be upheld only if it is necessary, and not merely rationally related to the accomplishment of a permissible state policy."[84] If the challenged statute limits political participation or free speech in the public affairs domain, it must pass "exacting scrutiny" by the Court, and its supporter must show "compelling" justification for it.[85] This seems to be the counterpart of the requirement stated by Chief Justice Waite, that successful rebuttal of the ordinary presumption of constitutionality must show invalidity "beyond a rational doubt."[86] The Court's opinions do not spell out with all desirable clarity the extent of the burden of justification put on the statute's supporter. What a showing of "necessity" or "compelling justification" seems usually to mean is a showing by the supporter that there is no reasonable alternative way to achieve a legitimate public-interest objective advanced in support of the act.[87] There are other constitutionally preferred values which do not call for so strong a showing by the proponent of the challenged statute. Thus where the regulation is not of speech in a political context, but of commercial advertising, the supporter must show that the act has a substantial relation to an important public-interest goal, and that it is no broader than needed to serve that goal, but this is enough.[88] A like requirement—less exacting than the "compelling justification" test—seems laid on one who supports a statutory classification according to sex.[89]

The scope appropriate to this essay does not allow reflecting the full elaboration of doctrine, the case-by-case movements, the differentiations developed by various Supreme Court justices that marked treatment of preferred-value analysis from the late 1930s on. This sketch is necessarily drawn in broad strokes; it does not purport to offer a guide sufficient for advising clients in particular situations. However, the sketch should indicate that these developments raise anew the old question of the legitimacy of judicial review of the constitutionality of legislation. The old question resurfaces especially as to the fifth of the preferred-value categories marked out by the Court since the 1930s. There is substantial warrant in the country's constitutional history for building a case for strict judicial scrutiny of legislation which makes invidious use of racial or analogous criteria to the detriment of historically disadvantaged groups, and of state legislation which discriminates against interstate commerce.[90] There is persuasive policy logic, though no specific historical base, for denying the presumption of constitutionality to legislation which burdens rational, representative lawmaking processes. The existence of such processes provides the base that warrants the presumption that a legislature has acted with fair, reasoned attention to the interests affected by a statute; a statute which cuts away at that base may well be deemed suspect.[91] Doctrine moves into more arguable ground when it applies strict scrutiny to legislation which limits communication in the arts or in the market. However, the Court's extension of special protection to communications processes outside the public affairs arena may be justified by concern that leniency toward encroaching legislation in the broader sphere might encourage spillover of restrictions into access to the vote and to political free speech.[92]

Most troublesome is enlarged judicial review on behalf of values of individual worth and dignity, viewed as invaded by laws regulating individual decisions on childbearing, or on sexual experience, or by laws which make sex the criterion for establishing legal rights, duties, or privileges. One may argue that such situations call for strict judicial scrutiny because they offer only variants of threats to interests disadvantaged by want of equal access to public policymaking processes.[93] However, since the Nineteenth Amendment, and given their proportion in the population, women cannot readily be classed as a politically disadvantaged minority. Special concern for protecting individual privacy in decisions on sex experience or childbearing by its own definition focuses on values outside the sphere of public policymaking.[94] One might counter that encroachments on individual privacy inherently pose political balance of power issues, because the individual who confronts social convention translated into law is likely to be at hopeless disadvantage unless strict judicial scrutiny somewhat redresses the imbalance. But this argument would warrant wholesale rejection of the presumption of constitutionality in a society so marked by the influence on public policy of organized groups as ours has become.[95] Moreover, statutes regulating conduct in the marketplace—to which the Court applies the presumption of constitutionality in full strength—often bring government power to bear on individuals and particular groups at the behest of special interests which enjoy superior skill and means in effecting their goals through legislation. In this perspective those who incur costs or burdens from much economic regulatory legislation might fairly claim to be politically disadvantaged in a degree not so different from the position of beneficiaries of the Court's preferred-value analysis.[96]

Popular feeling, political leaders, constitution makers, and legislators, as well as judges, have built into the country's constitutional tradition concern that public policy should respect the intrinsic worth and dignity of individuals. But it has never proved easy to achieve a firm consensus on what elements are essential to that valued individuality. Search for consensus has regularly encountered such differences of judgment and feeling as have persistently attended efforts to codify natural law.[97] These difficulties come to peculiarly sharp focus when we seek to legitimize the role of judges in displacing the normal primacy of legislative process in determining public policy. When we enlarge judicial review to protect preferred values of individuality we must calculate how much risk we should accept of translating into positive law the personal value standards of individual judges.

The constitutional crisis of the 1930s repudiated a large scope for exacting judicial review of "regulatory legislation affecting ordinary commercial transactions," and especially of laws trenching upon the preferred-value status which earlier decisions assigned to "freedom of contract."[98] But experience has blurred this apparently clear-cut demarcation of the proper limits of the judges' role. The harsh practice of modern totalitarian governments shows that by barring access to the job market or opportunity for the individual to exercise his special job skills law can as effectively police people's opinions and actions as it can through executions or concentration camps. The Supreme Court has recognized this reality in the concern it has given to defining substantive and procedural constitutional safeguards to access to jobs and to job holding.[99]

The extent of judicial discretion inherent in identifying preferred values of individuality is further underlined if we compare two lines of decisions regarding matters outside the market context. Rejecting the presumption of constitutionality, the Court required that the supporter show compelling justification for some statutes that punished abortion or the use of contraceptives; majorities of the Court viewed the individual's control of choice in bearing children as essential to proper respect for domains of life experience that should be private.[100] But the Court applied the presumption broadly on behalf of legislation that allocated limited public funds or other public economic assets.[101] It did so in favor of an appropriations act which denied public funds to pay for abortions desired by poor women.[102] It did so in favor of a statute which put a ceiling on the amount of public welfare money provided for poor families with children, refusing added funds for families with more than six children.[103] It did so on behalf of the broad discretion of a state legislature in determining the public funds to be available in support of public schools.[104] Cogent dissents by Justice Marshall argued that, no less than in the basic abortion and contraceptives cases, fundamental human rights were at stake in access to economic means to allow choice in childbearing, or to give access to food, clothing, and shelter needed to sustain life, or to provide education needed to achieve self-respecting status in the political process or in the job market.[105] Whether or not we agree with his plea to extend strict judicial scrutiny to public appropriations policy in these respects, his analysis highlights the extent of policymaking discretion inherent in the Court's rulings. In this field Court majorities in effect enforced a determination to hedge off the Court from direct involvement in effecting broad redistributions of wealth and income in the society, however much public spending decisions had impact on the quality of individual life.[106]

However we appraise the expansion of judicial review under the preferred-value analysis that has flourished since the late 1930s, we should not put it out of perspective. The values to which Court majorities have given constitutional preference carry high importance for free, rational political processes and for the worth of individual life. But we need to hold three qualifications in mind as we estimate the relative role of judges in the course taken by public policy. First, judges have not been the only actors on behalf of these values. Tardy and cumbersome as it tends to be, the legislative process has also contributed, as in legislation increasing access to public records, regulating use of money in politics, and enlarging legal protection of civil rights. Second, save in the limited instances in which constitutional rules apply, the presumption of constitutionality provides the frame within which the validity of the great bulk of legislation is judged; important as they are, preferred-value categories apply only to a small part of the whole body of statute law. Finally, contests in court carry drama which encourages people to exaggerate their range and incidence. The overwhelming bulk of statute law and the delegated legislation that exists within a framework of statute law never comes into any kind of constitutional litigation. Most legislative provisions for taxes, for public spending on services as well as on regulation, for regulating terms of dealing in market, for protecting public health and safety, for setting legal terms of incorporation and corporate finance, and for manifold other matters, put their considerable impress on the ongoing life of the society according to statutory standards and specifications, executive and administrative rules and orders, judicial interpretations, and advice which lawyers give to clients. Viewed against this sweep, even the important values to which the Court attaches preferred constitutional status are in play only in quite limited sectors of the whole legal order. However active our judges, they are a long way from judicializing the law of the late twentieth century.

NOTES

1. LEGISLATIVE PROCESS

1. Hurst 1950:23–34, 1977:35–37, 83.
2. Cary 1967, ch. 2; *cf.* United States v. United States District Court for the Eastern District of Michigan, 407 U.S. 297 (1972), and Youngstown Sheet & Tube Co. v. Sawyer, 343 U.S. 579 (1952) (court disinclined to accept existence of broad executive prerogative powers).
3. Gross 1953:166–70; Linde and Bunn 1976:131. *Cf* Jaffe 1965:461, 502, 508, 511–12, 517, 522; and Stewart 1975:1723, 1725, 1727, 1730, 1734–1738 (development of standing doctrine regarding litigation).
4. Nebbia v. New York, 291 U.S. 502, 536 (1934).
5. Silver v. Silver, 280 U.S. 117, 122 (1929); Noble State Bank v. Haskell, 219 U.S. 104, 113 (1911).
6. 61st Wisconsin Legislature, Assembly Journal, February 23, 1933, p. 423.
7. Goodland v. Zimmerman, 243 Wis. 459, 10 N.W.2d 180 (1943). *Cf.* Rose Manor Realty Co. v. Milwaukee, 272 Wis. 339, 75 N.W.2d 274 (1956) (court won't enjoin legislative process).
8. Maryland v. Wirtz, 392 U.S. 183, 190, n.13 (1968); Townsend v. Yeomans, 301 U.S. 441, 451 (1937); Powell v. Pennsylvania, 127 U.S. 678, 686 (1888).
9. Cohen 1952:34, 38–40; Linde and Bunn 1976:163–78.
10. Norwegian Nitrogen Products Co. v. United States, 288 U.S. 294, 315 (1933).
11. *Id.*, 304.
12. Watkins v. United States, 354 U.S. 178, 188 (1957); see United States v. Fort, 443 F.2d 670, 678 (1971), cert. den., 403 U.S. 932 (1971).
13. See e.g., Commonwealth v. Hunt, 45 Mass. (4 Metcalf) 111 (Mass. 1842) (presumptive legality of trade union activity). *Cf.* Tocqueville (1951) 2:325 (courts as offering special leverage to individuals and small groups).
14. Friedman 1973:384–96; Hurst 1977:143–54; Landis 1938:6–16, 34–37.

15. Friedman 1973:590; Freund 1917, chs. 1, 3.

16. Prosser 1971:190–204.

17. Kissinger v. Reporters Committee for Freedom of the Press, 445 U.S. 136, 148 (1980); Transamerica Mortgage Advisers, Inc. v. Lewis, 444 U.S. 11, 19 (1979); Touche Ross & Co. v. Redington, 442 U.S. 560, 568 (1979).

18. Cannon v. University of Chicago, 441 U.S. 677, 688 (1979); Cort v. Ash, 422 U.S. 66, 78 (1975); Sullivan v. Little Hunting Park, Inc., 396 U.S. 229 (1969); J. I. Case Co. v. Borak, 377 U.S. 426 (1964); Texas & New Orleans Railroad Co. v. Brotherhood of Railway & Steamship Clerks, 281 U.S. 548 (1930). *Cf.* Carlson v. Green, 446 U.S. 14, 18–20 (1980) (private action for damages for violation of constitutional rights).

19. Hurst 1977:120.

20. Duffy 1978:141–42, 151, 240, 275–79; Heller 1966:6–7, 20, 71, 74, 114; Lekachman 1966:196–97, 278–85; Lindblom 1977:177, 272–73.

21. On private associations: Hurst 1970:115–16. On official agencies, see Buckley v. Valeo, 424 U.S. 1, 125–33, 138–39 (1976); Morton v. Ruiz, 415 U.S. 199, 212 (1974); Barenblatt v. United States, 360 U.S. 109, 118–21 (1959); Allen v. Grand Central Aircraft Co. 347 U.S. 535, 544 (1954); Kendall v. United States, 37 U.S. (12 Peters) 524, 610, 613 (1838); Congressional Research Service (1973), 519–24. *Cf.* TVA v. Hill, 427 U.S. 153, 190 (1978) (appropriation does not override substantive statutory limit).

22. Beuscher 1941:1105; Letwin 1965:39–50; Thorelli 1955:38–48. *Cf.* People v. Fisher, 14 Wend. 9 (N.Y. Sup. Ct. Jud., 1835), and Commonwealth v. Hunt, 45 Mass. (4 Metcalf) 111 (1842) (differing approaches to conspiracy law applied to trade unions).

23. Friedman 1973:166–67, 172; Hurst 1970, *passim.*

24. Anderson 1973, ch. 4; Macaulay 1979:62, 63.

25. On general investigative authority: Sinclair v. United States, 279 U.S. 263, 291–92 (1929); McGrain v. Daugherty, 373 U.S. 135, 173–75 (1927). On judicial protection of free speech and assembly values: Gibson v. Florida Legislative Investigation Committee, 372 U.S. 539 (1963); *cf.* United States v. Rumely, 345 U.S. 41 (1953) (restrictive construction of House resolution authorizing lobby inquiry).

26. See Watkins v. United States, 354 U.S. 178, 188 (1957).

27. Gojack v. United States, 384 U.S. 702 (1966); Russell v. United States, 369 U.S. 749 (1962); Barenblatt v. United States, 360 U.S. 109 (1959); Watkins v. United States, 354 U.S. 178 (1957).

28. Hurst 1977:129–32.

29. Carosso 1970:151–55, 174–77, 180–81, 322–51, 368–72; Hurst 1974:11, 12–15, 22–24.

30. Freund 1917:192; Radin 1936:18–19; Walker 1934:12; see, e.g., Lewis Trucking Corporation v. Commonwealth of Virginia, 207 Va. 23, 29, 147 S.E.2d 747, 751–52 (1966); Bushnell v. Beloit, 10 Wis. 195, 225 (1860).

,o, 1949:1:64 (Bill of Rights, 1689) and 98 (Locke);
n legislative power).
–19; Hurst 1950:24–25, 30–32, 235.
58, 191–93; Hurst 1950:30–31.
66–71, 184–87; Tribe 1978:224–42, 247, 249–50.
:386–405, 419–25, 447, 456–61; Gunn 1980:270–74,
2–95; Heath 1954:357–67; Hurst 1950:51–62, 66–68.
ch. 15; Landis 1926:153; Potts 1926:691, 780; Walker

5–38.
:388–400, 661–68; Broude 1959:5–25; Scheiber 1969:353–60.
:134–72, 176–92.
965, chs. 1, 8, 13, 14, 16, 17; Hurst 1964:15–20, 62–93.
70, ch. 1 and 1977:175–77; White 1958, chs. 2, 3, 4, 5.
., United States v. American Trucking Associations, Inc., 310
(1940) Appalachian Coals, Inc. v. United States, 288 U.S. 344,

in 1957:29, 310–16; Hurst 1978:484–88.
win 1957:264–81, 286–88; Koenig 1964, chs. 6, 12; Neustadt 1964:43–54,
1, 154–55, 169–70.
ommittee on American Legislatures 1954:166–71, 198–99, 205, 207,

Committee on American Legislatures 1954:166, 167; Smithies 1955:67–89.
In general, see J. Chamberlain 1936:11–19, 450–64; L. Chamberlain
, chs. 1, 12; Gross 1953:99–103, 426–30; Redman 1973:16–17. *Cf.* Derthick
9:11, 43, 220, 229, 289, 304, and Witte 1962;3–12 (social security); Duffy
78:59, 190, and Miller 1980:367–72, 431–34 (civil rights).

48. Gross 1953, part 2.

49. J. W. Hampton, Jr. & Co. v. United States, 276 U.S. 394 (1928). *Cf.* Field v. Clark, 143 U.S. 649 (1892) (no invalid delegation where Congress authorizes executive action based on executive fact finding).

50. McCloskey 1960:166, 188; Tribe 1978:284–91. *Cf.* Davis 1969:44–51 (criticism and evaluation of courts' acceptance of lack of sufficient statutory standards in delegation).

51. See Bickel and Wellington 1957:38–39 (need for "remand" technique); *cf.* Industrial Union Department, AFL-CIO v. American Petroleum Institute, 100 Sup. Ct. 2844 (1980) (varied reactions to poorly defined delegation).

52. Linde and Bunn 1976:247–324, 586–635, 707–20.

53. Dodd and Schott 1979, *passim.*; Lowi 1969, chs. 4, 5.

54. Fenno 1966:681–92. See, e.g., Morton v. Ruiz, 415 U.S. 199, 228–29 (1974); Allen v. Grand Central Aircraft Co., 347 U.S. 535, 544 (1954).

55. E.g. Trans World Airlines, Inc. v. Hardison, 432 U.S. 63, 76, n.11 (1977);

Red Lion Broadcasting Co., Inc. v. FCC, 395 U.S. 367, 381–82 (1 State Construction Company v. Durkin, 345 U.S. 13, 16 (1953).

56. 60 Stat. 237 (1946), 5 U.S.C. sec. 551 (Federal Administrative Pr Act); Wis. Stat., 1977, ch. 227 (state Administrative Procedure Act).

57. United Housing Foundation, Inc. v. Forman, 421 U.S. 837, 848 Church of the Holy Trinity v. United States, 143 U.S. 457, 459–61 (1

58. See Cardozo, J., for the Court, in Norwegian Nitrogen Produc v. United States, 288 U.S. 294, 315 (1933).

59. *Cf.* Landis 1930:888–92, and Radin 1942:394, 410 (differing estima role of legislative history and statutory text). See, e.g., United States v. A ican Trucking Associations, Inc. 310 U.S. 534 (1940); Gooch v. United S 297 U.S. 124 (1936).

60. Tribe 1978, chs. 8, 11, 12, 15.

61. Freund 1917:208–14; Friedman 1973:301–2, 311–18, 489–94; H 1950:27–33, 73, 192–93, 229, 233, 409.

62. *The Federalist* (1907), 54.

63. Calhoun 1943:15.

64. Gross 1953:22–25, 93–100, 167–79, 284–94, 365–74, 382–89; Lanc 1930:888–92; Mayhew 1974:6–8, 33–38; Redman 1973:30–38.

65. Bolling 1966:135–37, 140–43, 221–30; Clapp 1963:313–20; Dahl an Lindblom 1953:320, 336–37, 340–41; Gross 1953:85–91, 338–63; Mayhev 1974:92–105, 111–31.

66. Handlin and Handlin 1947:44–48; Hurst 1978:522–34.

67. Friedman 1973:574–76, 586–91; Dahl and Lindblom 1953:320, 335, 338, 344, 526; Linde and Bunn 1976:68–96, 197–230; Truman 1951, chs. 11, 12, 16.

68. Hurst 1977:216–17.

69. Williamson v. Lee Optical of Oklahoma, Inc., 348 U.S. 483 (1955); Daniel v. Family Security Life Insurance Co., 336 U.S. 220 (1949); see Hurst 1978:526–33.

70. Tocqueville 1951:1:263–64, 2:9–10, 318–19.

71. Calhoun 1943:16.

72. Tribe 1978:298, 707–8.

73. Dodd and Schott 1979, *passim*; Lowi 1969:101–24; Thurow 1980:127–28.

74. Duffy 1978:28–50.

75. Braden v. United States 365 U.S. 431 (1961); Watkins v. United States, 354 U.S. 178 (1957); Sweezy v. New Hamphsire, 354 U.S. 234 (1957).

76. Clapp 1963:107–12; Gross 1953:175–77, 208–11, 359; Mayhew 1974:114–17, 122–31, 138–40.

77. Gross 1953:194–97; Thurow 1980:124–25.

78. Hurst 1950:38–40, 42–61, 95–101, 152, 199–203, 206–7, 210, and 1977:63–67, 129–32, 179–81, 185, 209–13.

79. Holmes 1881:106; Levy 1967:22, 24, 121, 129–35, 140–65, 187–91, 211–16, 290–95.

80. Mermin 1973:105–7.
81. Friedman 1973:569–75; Lowi 1969:30–32, 126–45; Truman 1951, ch. 14; Wooddy 1934:1274–1330.
82. Jaffe 1965:521, 565–67, 575, 600–4; Stewart 1975:1671, 1679, 1680, 1698–1702, 1711–1712, 1779, 1804, 1808.
83. Bunn and Gallagher 1977:965–70; Linde and Bunn 1976:591–634.

2. THE INTERPRETATION OF STATUTES

1. Gray 1909:119–20.
2. *Cf.* Wis. Stats, 1977, sec. 1.10 (a self-executing provision: ". . . the Wisconsin domestic animal is the dairy cow [*bos taurus*]").
3. Dickerson 1975:14–21, 242–50; Jones 1940:960–61.
4. Radin 1930:863. See Landis 1930:886. *Cf.* Radin 1942:388 (restatement of 1930 analysis with some qualifications).
5. Radin 1930:869–70.
6. *Cf. id.*, 878–79 (concession that statute law differs from judge-made law insofar as the statutory text sets "a maximum and a minimum of extension").
7. Holmes 1881:108, 123, 125.
8. 30 Co. 7a, 76 Eng. Rep. 637 (Exchequer, 1584).
9. Two of Radin's objections are relevant to difficulties in weighing evidence, but do not seem to negate the possibility of shared legislative intent. That we deal "with words which some two or three men drafted" raises problems of communication, but does not prove the impossibility of shared will on a proposition commonly understood; not every member of an assembly need put pen to paper to arrive at a common choice. That "a considerable number rejected" a proposed text does not negate the legal effect of the majority vote, though of course the presence of contending positions in consideration of the bill may create difficulties in determining how seriously to take remarks or propositions advanced in heat of combat.
10. Radin 1930;870.
11. *Ibid.*
12. Commonwealth v. Tilley, 306 Mass. 412, 28 N.E.2d 245 (1940). See Dickerson 1975:76, 128–31; Jones 1940:962–64.
13. Thorelli 1955:214–21; see Appalachian Coals, Inc. v. United States, 288 U.S. 344, 359–60 (1933) ("As a charter of freedom, the act has a generality and adaptability comparable to that found to be desirable in constitutional provisions").
14. White, CJ., for the Court in Standard Oil Co. v. United States, 221 U.S. 1, 69 (1911).
15. United States v. Trans-Missouri Freight Association, 166 U.S. 290 (1897); United States v. Paramount Pictures, Inc., 334 U.S. 131 (1948). See Jones 1940:968–69.

16. J. Chamberlain 1936:153–69; Fenno 1966, ch. 9, and pp. 590–614; Redman 1973:238–52.

17. Karnuth v. United States, 279 U.S. 231, 243 (1929). *Cf.* Healy v. Ratta, 292 U.S. 263, 269, 270 (1934) (restrictive interpretation of jurisdictional provision, based on analogous history).

18. Radin 1930:871.

19. Landis 1930:888.

20. Lanzetta v. New Jersey, 306 U.S. 451 (1939); United States v. L. Cohen Grocery Co., 255 U.S. 81 (1921).

21. Heydon's Case, 30 Co. 7a, 76 Eng. Rep. 637 (Exchequer, 1584); United States v. American Trucking Associations, Inc. 310 U.S. 534 (1940).

22. Radin 1930;875–76.

23. Patterson 1953:197–205.

24. 30 Co. 7a, 76 Eng. Rept. 637 (Exchequer, 1584).

25. *Cf.* Al-State Construction Co. v. Durkin, 345 U.S. 13, 16 (1953) (interweaving of original statute, administrative construction, and subsequent handling of statute in legislative hearings and by amendment); New York Central Railroad Co. v. White, 243 U.S. 188, 196–200 (1917) (law regarding industrial accident traced from common law to workers' compensation act to issue of constitutionality).

26. See Jackson, J., for the Court, in Securities and Exchange Commission v. C. J. Joiner Leasing Corporation, 320 U.S. 344, 350 (1943); Brandeis, J., for the Court, in Wright v. Vinton Branch of the Mountain Trust Bank, 300 U.S. 440, 463, n.8 (1937).

27. Erlenbaugh v. United States, 409 U.S. 239, 246, 248, n.23 (1972); United States v. Healy, 376 U.S. 75, 81 (1964).

28. Ross v. Ebert, 275 Wis. 523, 82 N.W.2d 315 (1957). Compare Wis. Laws, 1957 ch. 266, in which after more than a decade of experience in dealing with problems of racial discrimination the legislature added compulsory sanctions to the Code.

29. S & E Contractors, Inc. v. United States, 406 U.S. 1, 13, n.9 (1972). See United States v. Trans-Missouri Freight Association, 166 U.S. 290, 318 (1897).

30. Chicago & North Western Railway Co. v. United Transportation Union, 402 U.S. 570, 576 (1971). *Cf.* Church of the Holy Trinity v. United States, 143 U.S. 457, 464 (1892) (hearings show general purpose). See also, The Tap Line Cases, 234 U.S. 1, 27, (1914); The Delaware, 161 U.S. 459, 472 (1896) (recognition of link of legislation to groups particularly interested therein).

31. Wright v. Vinton Branch of the Mountain Trust Bank, 300 U.S. 440, 463, n.8 (1937); United States v. St. Paul, Minneapolis & Manitoba Railway Co., 247 U.S. 310, 318 (1918); see Learned Hand, circ. j., dissenting, in United States v. Ryan, 225 F.2d 417, 426–27 (2d circ. 1955).

32. See Jackson, J., concurring, in United States v. Public Utilities Commission of California, 345 U.S. 295, 319 (1953), and in Schwegemann Brothers v. Calvert Distillers Corporation, 341 U.S. 384, 395 (1951).

33. Healy v. Ratta, 292 U.S. 263, 269, 270 (1934). *Cf.* United States v. Cook, 384 U.S. 257 (1966), and City of Milwaukee v. Richards, 269 Wis. 570, 69 N.W.2d 445 (1955) (rule of strict construction of penal statutes yields before evidence of development of public policy by successive statutes).

34. See United States v. Pfitsch, 256 U.S. 547 (1921); Ross v. Ebert, 275 Wis. 523, 82 N.W.2d 315 (1957).

35. Norwegian Nitrogen Products Co. v. United States, 288 U.S. 294, 315 (1933).

36. Koshland v. Helvering, 298 U.S. 441, 446 (1936).

37. 143 U.S. 457 (1892).

39. 143 U.S. 457, 463–71 (1892).

40. E.g., United Housing Foundation, Inc. v. Forman, 421 U.S. 837, 848 (1975); Lynch v. Overholser, 369 U.S. 705, 710 (1962); Rathbun v. United States, 355 U.S. 107, 109 (1957).

41. Radin 1930:878–79.

42. Spaulding v. Chicago & Northwestern Railway Co., 30 Wis. 110, 116, 120 (1872). *Cf.* Oshkosh City Railway Co. v. Winnebago County, 89 Wis 435, 439, 61 N.W. 1107, 1108 (1895) (street railway not liable for assessment for paving between its tracks under statute authorizing city to "charge the cost [of the paving] . . . to the center of the street . . . to any lot or lots fronting or abutting on such street . . . :" "Waiving all question of strict or liberal construction, the court must, at least, be able to see in the words used a legislative intention to make the plaintiff's right of way liable to the assessment").

43. Church of the Holy Trinity v. United States, 143 U.S. 457, 458–59, 463–65 (1892).

44. Commonwealth v. Tilley, 306 Mass. 412, 28 N.E.2d 245 (1940); People v. Hines, 284 N.Y. 93, 29 N.E.2d 483 (1940); State v. Gould, 56 Wis 2d 808, 202 N.W.2d 903 (1973); State v. Hartfiel, 24 Wis. 60 (1869).

45. United States v. Trans-Missouri Freight Association, 166 U.S. 290, 316, 320 (1897).

46. Church of the Holy Trinity v. United States, 143 U.S. 457, 459 (1892). *Cf.* McKenna, J., dissenting, in Caminetti v. United States, 242 U.S. 470, 500 (1917) (dangers of mechanical enforcement of full verbal scope of statute).

47. Church of the Holy Trinity v. United States, 143 U.S. 457, 463 (1892). See Jones 1940:971–72.

48. Townsend v. Yeomans, 301 U.S. 441, 452 (1937); Cartwright v. Sharpe, 40 Wis 2d 494, 508–9, 162 N.W.2d 5, 12 (1968).

49. Assured resort to extrinsic materials dates from the twentieth century. *Cf.* United States v. Trans-Missouri Freight Association, 166 U.S. 290, 318 (1897) (intimation of English doctrine); Federal Trade Commission v. Raladam

Co., 283 U.S. 643, 649 (1931) (tentative broadening of acceptance of extrinsic material); Wright v. Vinton Branch of the Mountain Trust Bank, 300 U.S. 440, 463, n.8 (1937) (general acceptance).

50. See Viscount Haldane, in Viscountess Rhondda's Claim (1922) 2 A.C. 339, 383–84 (H.L.); Farwell LJ., in The King v. The County Council of the West Riding of Yorkshire (1906) 2 K.B. 676, (Ct. App.); *cf.* Frankfurter, J., dissenting in Commissioner of Internal Revenue v. Acker, 361 U.S. 87, 94 (1959) (noting continuance of English rule in contrast to doctrine in the United States). See, generally, Dickerson (1975):161–62, 168, 170–74, 195.

51. Heydon's Case, 30 Co. 7a, 76 Eng. Rep. 637 (Exchequer, 1584).

52. Jackson 1948:535, 537–38.

53. *Ibid.*

54. See Jackson, J., concurring, in United States v. Public Utilities Commission of California, 345 U.S. 295, 319 (1953), and in Schwegemann Brothers v. Calvert Distillers Corporation, 341 U.S. 384, 395 (1951).

55. See United States v. Trans-Missouri Freight Association, 166 U.S. 290, 318 (1897); *cf.* Linde and Bunn (1976):364–66 (on the manufacture of legislative history).

56. United States v. Hartwell, 73 U.S. (6 Wallace) 385, 396 (1868).

57. United States v. Shreveport Grain & Elevator Co., 287 U.S. 77, 83 (1932), quoting Hamilton v. Rathbone, 175 U.S. 414, 421 (1899).

58. United States v. Shreveport Grain & Elevator Co., 287 U.S. 77, 84 (1932).

59. See United States v. Healy, 376 U.S. 75, 83–85 (1964); Federal Trade Commission v. Raladam Co., 283 U.S. 643, 649 (1931); Church of the Holy Trinity v. United States, 143 U.S. 457, 459, 463–65 (1892); In re Adoption of Shields, 4 Wis. 2d 219, 223, 89 N.W.2d 827, 830 (1958).

60. Boston Sand & Gravel Co. v. United States, 278 U.S. 41, 48 (1928). Accord: Harrison v. Northern Trust Co., 317 U.S. 476, 479 (1943); United States v. American Trucking Associations, Inc., 310 U.S. 534, 543–44 (1940).

61. United States v. Dotterweich, 320 U.S. 277, 282 (1943); Gooch v. United States, 297 U.S. 124, 128 (1936).

62. Llewellyn 1960:521–29.

63. Church of the Holy Trinity v. United States, 143 U.S. 457, 458 (1892).

64. Baltimore & Ohio Railway Co. v. Jackson, 353 U.S. 325, 331 (1957). Accord: United States v. Healy, 376 U.S. 75, 83 (1964); Securities and Exchange Commission v. C. M. Joiner Leasing Corporation, 320 U.S. 344, 351 (1943).

65. Nix v. Hedden, 149 U.S. 304 (1893). See Addison v. Holly Hill Fruit Products, Inc., 322 U.S. 607, 618 (1944). *Cf.* Cadwalader v. Zeh, 151 U.S. 171, 176, 178 (1894) (proof of specialized trade usage prevails).

66. Caminetti v. United States, 242 U.S. 470, 486 (1917).

67. See Lynd and Lynd 1929:112–13.

68. See McKenna, J., dissenting, in Caminetti v. United States, 242 U.S.

470, 497–98 (1917). The statutory context—the reference to "debauchery" as well as to "prostitution"—provides some basis for arguing that Congress was addressing a broader subject than commericialized sex. See Cleveland v. United States, 329 U.S. 14, 17 (1946) (appeal to "common understanding" of "debauchery"). But some question begging remains. This broader reading is still irrelevant to the question, was Congress in the Mann Act addressing the subject of all illicit sex, including casual episodes. See Black, Jackson, and Rutledge, JJ., dissenting, 329 U.S. 21, 22 (1946).

69. Chemehuevi Tribe of indians v. Federal Power Commission, 420 U.S. 395, 403 (1975); United States v. Concentrated Phosphate Export Association, Inc., 393 U.S. 199, 207 (1968).

70. 297 U.S. 124 (1936).

71. *Id.*, 129.

72. Kokoszka v. Belford, 417 U.S. 642, 650 (1974); Brotherhood of Railroad Trainmen v. Jacksonville Terminal Co., 394 U.S. 369, 383–84 (1969).

73. Gooch v. United States, 297 U.S. 124, 126–27 (1936).

74. United States v. American Trucking Associations, Inc., 310 U.S. 534, 544–45 (1940). *Cf.* Morris v. McComb, 332 U.S. 422 (1947) (reflecting fact that Congress did not change the pattern of law defined under the principal case).

75. For intimations that statutory change in common law must be express, see, e.g., Robert C. Herd & Co., Inc. v. Krawill Machinery Corporation, 359 U.S. 297, 305 (1959); Pearson v. School District No. 8, 144 Wis. 620, 622, 129 N.W. 940, 941 (1911). More typical are statements allowing changes in common law by statutory implication, as in Wicks v. City of Charlottesville, 215 Va. 274, 276, 208 S.E.2d 752, 755 (1974); Sullivan v. School District No. 1, 179 Wis. 502, 506, 191 N.W. 1020, 1022 (1923).

76. Rebuttal of derogation rule on showing of sharp statutory change of policy premises: Allen v. People, 175 Colo. 113, 185 P.2d 886 (1971); Anderson v. Miller Scrap Iron Co., 169 Wis. 106, 170 N.W. 275 (1919). Rebuttal of penal statute rule on showing of trend of successive statutes and legislative history: Gooch v. United States, 297 U.S. 124 (1936); City of Milwaukee v. Richards, 269 Wis. 570, 69 N.W.2d 445 (1955).

77. See, e.g., Lane v. State, 120 Neb. 302, 232 N.W. 96 (1930) (penal statute rule); Meek v. Pierce, 19 Wis. 300 (1865) (derogation rule).

78. *Cf.* Fletcher v. Peck, 10 U.S. (6 Cranch) 87, 139 (1810), and Ives v. South Buffalo Railway Co., 201 N.Y. 271, 293–94, 298, 94 N.E. 431, 439–40 (1911) (intimations of established judge-made law as substantive limitations on legislative power). But see Goldblatt v. Town of Hempstead, 369 U.S. 590, 593 (1962); New York Central Railroad Co. v. White, 243 U.S. 188, 198 (1917) (repudiating common law as fixed element of substantive due process).

79. Securities and Exchange Commission v. C. M. Joiner Leasing Corporation, 320 U.S. 344, 350 (1943). See Jones 1940:958.

80. See, e.g., Rogers v. Donovan, 268 Ore. 24, 518 P.2d 1306 (1974); Black-

man v. Iles, 4 N.J. 82, 71 A.2d 633 (1950); Schneider v. C. M. & St. P. Ry. Co., 99 Wis 378, 75 N.W. 169 (1898).

81. McBoyle v. United States, 283 U.S. 25 (1931); Highway Trailer Co. v. Janesville Electric Co. 187 Wis. 161, 204 N.W. 773 (1925).

82. Contrast restrictive construction of penal statutes in State v. Read, 162 Iowa 572, 144 N.W. 310 (1913), and State ex rel. Wisconsin Registration Board of Architects and Professional Engineers v. T.V. Engineers of Kenosha, Inc., 30 Wis. 2d 434, 141 N.W.2d 235 (1966) (regulations affecting economic dealings ordinarily acceptable), with the absence of reference to strict construction of penal statutes in broad application of legislation in Commonwealth v. Tilley, 306 Mass. 412, 28 N.E.2d 245 (1940) (theft), and State v. Hartfiel, 24 Wis. 60 (1869) (sale of liquor to minors).

83. Holmes, J., for the Court, in United States v. Jin Fuey Moy, 241 U.S. 394, 402 (1916).

3. THE CONSTITUTIONALITY OF STATUTES

1. Hurst 1978:494–95. See United States v. Butler, 297 U.S. 1, 64–67 (1936).

2. *Cf.* Hand 1959:144 (vitality of constitutional principles depends on general community response, not just on formal agencies of law).

3. See Ferguson v. Skrupa, 372 U.S. 726, 730–32 (1963).

4. See Holmes 1881:1, 123–27 (judges as policy originators), and Holmes, J., for the Court, in Noble State Bank v. Haskell, 219 U.S. 104, 113 (1911) (legislators as policy originators). *Cf.* Holmes, J., dissenting, in Lochner v. New York, 198 U.S. 45, 75 (1905) (criticizing judges for departing from reviewing into originating role in judicial review).

5. Hand, circ. j., for the court, in Borden's Farm Products Co., Inc. v. Ten Eyck, 11 Fed. Supp. 599, 600 (S.D.N.Y., 1935). For implicit validations of Judge Hand's analysis, see Brotherhood of Locomotive Firemen and Enginemen v. Chicago, Rock Island & Pacific Railroad Co., 393 U.S. 129, 139 (1968); South Carolina State Highway Department v. Barnwell Brothers, Inc., 303 U.S. 177, 191–92 (1938); see, also, Holmes, J., for the Court, in Laurel Hill Cemetery v. City and County of San Francisco, 216 U.S. 358, 365 (1910). The presumption of constitutionality is applied, also, to policy generalizations made within their delegated jurisdiction by subordinate legislative bodies, including those of municipal governments and administrative agencies. See Brandeis, J., for the Court, in Pacific States Box & Basket Co. v. White, 296 U.S. 176, 185, 186 (1935). Where the constitutional question turns on underlying questions of fact and fact-involved values outside the domain of legal expertise the same utilitarian reason (of informing the judges) obtains as where a statute is in issue. And the Court appears to find basis for judicial deference to determinations by these bodies, though of subordinate legal status, because they are delegates of the legislature.

6. See Hand, circ. j., in Borden's Farm Products Co., Inc. v. Ten Eyck, 11 Fed. Supp. 599, 600 (S.D.N.Y., 1935).

7. *Cf.* Holmes 1881:102, 114–15, 123–24 (jury's role in finding facts and making value judgments in areas courts find open to debate).

8. Jaffe 1965:521, 565–67, 575, 600, 603, 604. *Cf.* Stewart 1975;1670, 1679, 1680, 1698–1702, 1711, 1723, 1779, 1804, 1808 (limited judicial review of particular administrative action, coupled with late twentieth-century tendency for closer judicial review of terms of access of interests to processes of administrative policy generalization).

9. John F. Jelke Co. v. Emery, 193 Wis. 311, 321–22, 214 N.W. 369, 373 (1927).

10. *Ibid.*

11. *Cf.* International Harvester Credit Corporation v. Goodrich, 350 U.S. 537, 547 (1956); Nebbia v. New York, 291 U.S. 502, 537 (1934); Silver v. Silver, 280 U.S. 117, 122 (1929); Proprietors of the Charles River Bridge v. Proprietors of the Warren Bridge, 36 U.S. (11 Peters) 420, 548 (1837); Fletcher v. Peck, 10 U.S. (6 Cranch) 87, 135 (1810) (various forms of recognition of scope for legislative innovation in public policy).

12. McCulloch v. Maryland, 17 U.S. (4 Wheaton) 316 (1819).

13. Richardson 1896:2:576, 582.

14. *Id.*, 576, 583, 589.

15. (1913) 49 Cong. Rec. (pt. 5) 4291, 4292; 63d Cong., 1st Sess., S. Doc. No. 103, p. 6.

16. Act of March 1, 1913, 37 Stat. 699; 49 Cong. Rec. (pt. 5) 4299, 4447.

17. 74th Cong., 1st Sess., (1935) 79 Cong. Rec. (pt. 12) 13449.

18. Act of August 30, 1935, c. 82, 49 Stat. 991. The labor relations provisions were held invalid as exceeding the commerce power and constituting a forbidden delegation of legislative power in Carter v. Carter Coal Co., 298 U.S. 238 (1936); the price-fixing provisions were interpreted to be inseparable from the invalid portions and so not to be operative. Hughes, CJ., agreeing with the ruling on the labor provisions, found the price-fixing provisions separable and within Congress's power. Cardozo, J., joined by Brandeis and Stone, JJ., dissented, finding the price-fixing provisions separable and valid, and the issues regarding the labor provisions prematurely raised.

19. See remarks of Representative Lenroot, March 1, 1913, 49 Cong. Rec. (pt. 5) 4446, in contrast to those of Representative Stanley, *id.*, 4441.

20. See note 16, *supra*, on the Webb Kenyon Act. Carter v. Carter Coal Co., 298 U.S. 238 (1936) was in substance overruled by National Labor Relations Board v. Jones & Laughlin Steel Corporation, 301 U.S. 1 (1937).

21. See notes 5, 6, *supra*, and accompanying text.

22. 127 U.S. 678 (1888).

23. The presumption of constitutionality was successfully rebutted in later decisions regarding such statutory bans on oleomargarine. See the discussion

of the course of doctrine in John F. Jelke Co. v. Emery, 193 Wis. 311, 214 N.W. 369 (1927).

24. See, e.g., Abood v. Detroit Board of Education, 431 U.S. 209 (1977); Usery v. Turner Elkhorn Mining Co., 428 U.S. 1 (1976); Williamson v. Lee Optical of Oklahoma, Inc., 348 U.S. 483 (1955).

25. 127 U.S. 678, 684 (1888).

26. *Id.*, 685–86.

27. See Tribe 1978:234–37 ("empirical" approach to defining scope of commerce power), 451 (continued focus on public interest justifications under due process criteria). *Cf.* Miller, J., for the Court, in Davidson v. Board of Administrators of the City of New Orleans, 96 U.S. 97, 104 (1878) (due process clause best defined "by the gradual process of judicial inclusion and exclusion, as the cases presented for decision shall require"), and Holmes, J., for the Court, in Galveston, Harrisburg & San Antonio Ry. Co. v. Texas, 210 U.S. 217, 225 (1908) ("Regulation and commerce among the States both are practical rather than technical conceptions, and naturally, their limits must be fixed by practical lines.").

28. Home Building & Loan Association v. Blaisdell, 290 U.S. 398, 426 (1934).

29. See Powell v. Pennsylvania, 127 U.S. 678, 685–86 (1888); see notes 5 and 6 *supra*, and accompanying text.

30. U.S. Constitution, Article I, sections 9, 10

31. See Cummings v. Missouri, 71 U.S. (4 Wallace) 277, 319, 320 (1867); Tribe (1978) 480–84.

32. In re Medley, 134 U.S. 160 (1890); Kring v. Missouri, 108 U.S. 221 (1883). But *cf.* Harisiades v. Shaughessy, 342 U.S. 580, 594–95 (1952) (retroactive criteria for deportation not within ex post facto clause).

33. Hawker v. New York, 170 U.S. 189 (1898). Analogous is DeVeau v. Braisted, 363 U.S. 144 (1960).

34. U.S. Constitution, Article I, section 10.

35. Dartmouth College v. Woodward, 17 U.S. (4 Wheaton) 518 (1819); Fletcher v. Peck, 10 U.S. (6 Cranch) 87 (1810).

36. Home Building & Loan Association v. Blaisdell, 290 U.S. 398, 435, 437, 438 (1934).

37. Where the supporter has made a prima facie case that the prime purpose of a retroactive statute is not to rearrange prior bargains among the parties, but to serve some non-market public interest—such as protection of public morals or public health—the Court seems in effect if not in plain language to apply the presumption of constitutionality. This is the meaning of decisions which invoke the formula that a state may not contract away its police power. Stone v. Mississippi, 101 U.S. 814, 817, 818–19, 821 (1880); Fertilizing Co. v. Hyde Park, 97 U.S. 659, 667 (1879). Where the issue arises because of retroactive change of remedies for enforcing contracts, though the Court concedes

some scope for legislative discretion to change patterns of remedies, the judges seem typically to decide the gravity of the change simply from their own knowledge as legal experts, without invoking the presumption; in twentieth-century opinions which introduce attention to environing facts of business practice or economic impact, the tone is nonetheless to require that the supporter of the statute make a positive showing for it. El Paso v. Simmons, 379 U.S. 497, 511–13, 516 (1965); East New York Savings Bank v. Hahn, 326 U.S. 230, 233, 234 (1945); Veix v. Sixth Ward Building & Loan Association of Newark, 310 U.S. 32, 37, 38–39, 41 (1940). Where the challenger shows from the terms of the challenged act or from its likely effect that its immediate purpose is to restructure existing bargains as such, even if for some more remote public interest goal, it is plain that the contract clause operates to require of the supporter what amounts to a showing of "compelling" justification. This is especially so if the fiscal capacities of the government itself stand to benefit from the change. United States Trust Co. v. New Jersey, 431 U.S. 1, 24, 26 (1977); Missouri, Kansas & Texas Ry. Co. v. Oklahoma, 271 U.S. 303 (1926); Grand Trunk Western Ry. Co. v. City of South Bend, 227 U.S. 544 (1913). See, also, State ex rel. Building Owners & Managers Association of Milwaukee, Inc. v. Adamany, 64 Wis. 2d 280, 219 N.W.2d 274 (1974).

38. Berger 1977:194–200, 232, 241, 259.

39. 95 U.S. 714, 722–26, 733–35 (1877). This aspect of the opinion is highlighted by contrast with the dissent of Hunt, J., which seems to treat the question in issue as one to which a presumption of constitutionality approach was appropriate. *Id.*, 737. Analogous to the "rule" approach taken in Pennoyer v. Neff is the Court's treatment of Harris v. Balk, 198 U.S. 215, 222 (1905), setting the conditions for a valid judgment quasi in rem.

40. Smith v. Organization of Foster Families for Equality and Reform, 431 U.S. 816, 855 (1977). A broader turn away from the "rule" approach of Pennoyer v. Neff may be signaled by Shaffer v. Heitner, 433 U.S. 186, 206, 208, 212 (1977).

41. Fletcher v. Peck, 10 U.S. (6 Cranch) 87, 128 (1810).

42. O'Gorman & Young, Inc. v. Hartford Fire Insurance Co., 282 U.S. 251, 256–58 (1931); Lindsley v. Natural Carbonic Gas Co., 220 U.S. 61, 78–80 (1911).

43. See note 5 and accompanying text, *supra*.

44. See Cummings v. Missouri, 71 U.S. (4 Wallace) 277, 319, 320 (1867). For analogous handling of the burden of persuasion under constitutional rules, see United States v. Lovett, 328 U.S. 303, 313, 316–17 (1946) (ban on bills of attainder); Thompson v. Utah, 170 U.S. 343, 353 (1898). Controversial changes that the Court later made in defining the substantive content of the guaranty of jury trial involved in *Thompson* do not deny continued relevance to the

approach there indicated in applying a constitutional rule. See Harlan, J., dissenting, in Williams v. Florida, 399 U.S. 78, 122, 126 (1970).

45. Powell v. Pennsylvania, 127 U.S. 678, 681–82 (1888). Consider in the light of this state of the record the significance (for establishing the base of the presumption) of the observation by Harlan, J., for the Court, that "the legislature of Pennsylvania, upon the fullest investigation, as we must conclusively presume, and upon reasonable grounds, as must be assumed from the record, has determined that the prohibition of the sale . . . [of oleomargarine] will promote the public health . . ." Accord, that the existence of the statute suffices to provide the base of the presumption of constitutionality, see, e.g., Commonwealth v. Davis, 369 Mass., 886, 889, 343 N.E.2d 847, 850 (1976); Shelton College v. State Board of Education, 48 N.J. 501, 506, 226 A.2d 612, 615 (1967); State v. Stehlek, 262 Wis. 642, 645, 56 N.W.2d 514, 516 (1953).

46. Carmichael v. Southern Coal & Coke Co., 301 U.S. 495, 510 (1937); Pinnick v. Cleary, 360 Mass. 1, 28, 271 N.E.2d 592, 609 (1971); Rosenthal v. Hartnett, 36 N.Y. 2d 269, 273, 326 N.E.2d 811, 813 (1975). *Cf.* Maryland v. Wirtz, 392 U.S. 183, 190, n.13 (1968); Townsend v. Yeomans, 301 U.S. 441, 451 (1937) (no judicially enforcible requirement of procedural due process, that a legislature conduct a special investigation or make explicit findings before it legislates).

47. National power to tax and spend: Steward Machine Co. v. Davis, 301 U.S. 548, 584 (1937); Helvering v. Davis, 301 U.S. 619, 640 (1937). National power to regulate commerce: Wickard v. Filburn, 317 U.S. 111, 127–28 (1942); United States v. Darby, 312 U.S. 100, 114, 115 (1941).

48. West Coast Hotel Co. v. Parrish, 300 U.S. 379, 400 (1937); Nebbia v. New York, 291 U.S. 502, 537 (1934).

49. Regarding alleged nondiscriminatory burdens on interstate commerce: South Carolina State Highway Department v. Barnwell Brothers, Inc., 303 U.S. 177, 191–92 (1938); Southern Railway Co. v. King, 217 U.S. 524, 536 (1910), with which compare Seaboard Air Line Railway v. Blackwell, 244 U.S. 310, 312, 313 (1917) (presumption found rebutted, regarding same act). But *cf.* Raymond Motor Transportation, Inc. v. Rice, 434 U.S. 429, 440, 443, 444–45 (1978), and Bibb v. Navajo Freight Lines, Inc., 359 U.S. 520, 528–29 (1959) (burden of persuasion shifted to supporter of state statute shown by challenger to erect a specifically identifiable legal or factual barrier physically impeding interstate commerce).

50. American Power & Light Co. v. Securities and Exchange Commission, 329 U.S. 90, 105 (1946); United States v. Rock Royal Co-operative, Inc., 307 U.S. 533, 574 (1939); Buttfield v. Stranahan, 192 U.S. 470, 492 (1904).

51. E.g., Patterson v. New York, 432 U.S. 197, 210 (1977) (statutory allocation of burden of proof on defense to establish affirmative defense in criminal proceedings); Usery v. Turner Elkhorn Mining Co., 428 U.S. 1, 33–34 (1976)

(statutory rule of evidence in workers' compensation cases); Massachusetts Board of Retirement v. Murgia, 427 U.S. 307, 314 (1976) (mandatory retirement age of police); Shilb v. Kuebel, 404 U.S. 357, 364 (1971) (statutory provision for administrative costs of bail system); United States v. National Dairy Products Corporation, 372 U.S. 29, 32–33 (1963) (issue of vagueness of penal statute regulating business).

52. 127 U.S. 678, 684 (1888), quoting Waite, CJ., for the Court, in The Sinking Fund Cases, 99 U.S. 700, 718 (1879).

53. See, e.g., Vance v. Bradley, 440 U.S. 93, 97 (1979); Olsen v. Nebraska, 313 U.S. 236, 246 (1941); Lawrence v. State Tax Commission of Mississippi, 286 U.S. 276, 283 (1932); Lindsley v. Natural Carbonic Gas Co., 220 U.S. 61, 78 (1911).

54. See, e.g., Brotherhood of Locomotive Firemen & Enginemen v. Chicago, Rock Island & Pacific R.R. Co., 393 U.S. 129, 136, 137 (1968); Powell v. Texas, 392 U.S. 514, 522, 526, 535 (1968); Borden's Farm Products Co. v. Ten Eyck, 297 U.S. 251, 261 (1936); Laurel Hill Cemetery v. City and County of San Francisco, 216 U.S. 358, 364–66 (1910); Jacobson v. Massachusetts, 197 U.S. 11, 30 (1905).

55. Powell v. Pennsylvania, 127 U.S. 678, 682 (1888).

56. 293 U.S. 163 (1934).

57. *Id.*, 170. Accord: Williamson v. Lee Optical of Oklahoma, Inc., 348 U.S. 483, 486, 487–88 (1955); Tennessee Electric Power Co. v. Tennessee Valley Authority, 306 U.S. 118, 139 (1939); Morris v. Duby 274 U.S. 135, 144 (1927).

58. Usery v. Turner Elkhorn Mining Co., 428 U.S. 1, 16 (1976); Chase Securities Corporation v. Donaldson, 325 U.S. 304, 315–16 (1945); Welch v. Henry, 305 U.S. 134, 144 (1938).

59. Noble State Bank v. Haskell, 219 U.S. 104, 113 (1911). Accord: Goldblatt v. Town of Hempstead, 369 U.S. 590, 593 (1962); Silver v. Silver, 280 U.S. 117, 122 (1929); New York Central R.R. Co. v. White, 243 U.S. 188, 198 (1917).

60. Ferguson v. Skrupa, 372 U.S. 726 (1963); Railway Express Agency, Inc. v. New York, 336 U.S. 106 (1949); Roschen v. Ward, 279 U.S. 337 (1929); Miller v. Schoene, 276 U.S. 272 (1928). But some decisions seem to say that if the challenger makes a prima facie showing of special private gain from a statute, the court may require the supporter to go forward with substantial evidence to show the presence of a concurrent public interest. See Roberts, J., for a 6–3 majority, in Mayflower Farms, Inc. v. Ten Eyck, 297 U.S. 266, 272, 274 (1936), and the sharp dissent there by Cardozo, J., joined by Brandeis and Stone, JJ., *id.*, 275, 278.

61. Powell v. Pennsylvania, 127 U.S. 678, 684, 685 (1888).

62. Vance v. Bradley, 440 U.S. 93, 102, 106 (1979); Goldblatt v. Town of Hempstead, 369 U.S. 590, 595 (1962); Williamson v. Lee Optical of Oklahoma, Inc., 348 U.S. 483, 486, 487–88 (1955); Carolene Products Co. v. United States,

323 U.S. 18, 28–29 (1944); Missouri, Kansas & Texas Ry. Co. v. May, 194 U.S. 267, 270 (1904). But see Mayflower Farms, Inc. v. Ten Eyck, 297 U.S. 266, 272, 274, and Cardozo, J., dissenting (joined by Brandeis and Stone, JJ.), 278 (1936); Currie, J., dissenting in Town of Caledonia v. Racine Limestone Co., Inc., 266 Wis. 475, 481, 488, 63 N.W.2d 697, 700, 703 (1954).

63. Powell v. Pennsylvania, 127 U.S. 678, 686 (1888).

64. See Hughes, CJ., for the Court, in Borden's Farm Products Co. v. Baldwin, 293 U.S. 194, 209 (1934) (presumption does not mean "treating any fanciful conjecture as enough to repel attack.").

65. Fleming v. Nestor, 363 U.S. 603, 612 (1960). See, also, decisions ruling that there is no requirement that the statute on its face declare its rationale, or that there be a legislative record or formal findings in support of the act. Note 46, *supra*. *Cf.* State ex rel. LaFollette v. Torphy, 85 Wis. 2d 94, 102, 270 N.W.2d 187, 190 (1978) ("The reason the legislature included this provision is irrelevant as long as the court cannot say that 'no state of facts can reasonably be conceived that would sustain it'"). But see dissent of Powell, J. (joined by Brennan, Marshall, and Stevens, JJ.) in Schweiker v. Wilson, 101 Sup. Ct. 1074, 1088 (1981), suggesting that if neither the statutory text nor legislative history present a clearly declared, plausible rationale for a challenged statute, the court should require the supporter to advance an explanation that bears a "fair and substantial relation" to such purpose as the supporter claims for the act. The dissent acknowledges and does not repudiate Fleming v. Nestor, but seems to qualify it by some shift in the burden of going forward with argument.

66. See Johnson v. Robison, 415 U.S. 361, 376 (1974); United States Department of Agriculture v. Moreno, 413 U.S. 528, 534–35 (1973). See, also, Stevens, J., concurring, in Califano v. Goldfarb, 430 U.S. 199, 213 (1977); Brennan, J., dissenting in Schlesinger v. Ballard, 419 U.S. 498, 520 (1975). *Cf.* United States v. Romano, 382 U.S. 136, 144 (1965); Tot v. United States, 319 U.S. 463, 472 (1953); Smith v. Cahoon, 283 U.S. 553 (1931) (decisions apparently restricting possible justification to that indicated on face of challenged statutes).

67. United States v. Carolene Products Co., 304 U.S. 144, 152 (1938).

68. O'Gorman and Young, Inc. v. Hartford Fire Insurance Co., 282 U.S. 251, 257–58 (1931). The challenger lost on his demurrer or like motion in Day-Brite Lighting, Inc. v. Missouri, 342 U.S. 421, 425 (1952); Olsen v. Nebraska, 313 U.S. 236, 246 (1941); United States v. Darby, 312 U.S. 100, 108, 115, 120 (1941); United States v. Carolene Products Co., 304 U.S. 144, 154 (1938).

69. Borden's Farm Products Co. v. Baldwin, 293 U.S. 194, 213 (1934); see s.c., sub nom., Borden's Farm Products Co., Inc., v. Ten Eyck, 11 Fed. Supp. 599 (S.D.N.Y. 1935), 297 U.S. 251 (1936). Of like character are United States v. International Union, UAW-CIO, 352 U.S. 567, 591–92 (majority), 595–98 (dissent) (1957); Gibbs v. Buck, 307 U.S. 66, 76 (1939); Polk Co. v. Glover, 305 U.S. 5, 10 (1938); Chastleton Corporation v. Sinclair, 264 U.S. 543, 548 (1924).

70. Pacific States Box & Basket Co. v. White, 296 U.S. 176, 184–85 (1935). See, also, Pierce Oil Corporation v. City of Hope, 248 U.S. 498, 500 (1919); Southern R.R. Co. v. King, 217 U.S. 524, 536 (1910).

71. Note the unacknowledged use of judicial notice by majority and dissent in O'Gorman and Young, Inc. v. Hartford Fire Insurance Co., 282 U.S. 251, 257, 267 (1931), as well as the implicit doubt raised as to the propriety of such invocation on both sides, since majority and dissent in effect took judicial notice of diametrically opposed propositions of fact. *Cf.* Board of Education v. Allen, 392 U.S. 236, 248 (1968) and Lemon v. Kurtzman, 403 U.S. 602, 617 (1971) (rejection of judicial notice, and allowance of it on closely similar subjects); New State Ice Co. v. Liebman, 285 U.S. 262, 278, 289–90 (1932) (judicial notice taken by majority and dissent for propositions essentially in conflict). State v. Kerndt, 274 Wis. 113, 115, 79 N.W.2d 113, 114 (1956) offers an example of commendable restraint in rejecting an attack on the validity of a statute based on an appeal to judicial notice.

72. E.g., McKeiver v. Pennsylvania, 403 U.S. 528, 548 (1971); West Coast Hotel v. Parrish, 300 U.S. 379, 399 (1937); Block v. Hirsh, 256 U.S. 135, 154 (1921); Red "C" Oil Manufacturing Co. v. Board of Agriculture of North Carolina, 222 U.S. 380, 392 (1912).

73. Care is taken to frame reference to judicial notice in these negative terms in O'Gorman and Young, Inc. v. Hartford Fire Insurance Co., 282 U.S. 251, 258 (1931), and in Powell v. Pennsylvania, 127 U.S. 678, 684 (1888).

74. See, e.g., Ferguson v. Skrupa, 372 U.S. 726 (1963); Williamson v. Lee Optical of Oklahoma, Inc. 348 U.S. 483 (1955).

75. Contrast Mahan v. Howell, 410 U.S. 315 (1973) (presumption of constitutionality applied regarding state statute apportioning legislative districts for state legislature) with Kirkpatrick v. Preisler, 394 U.S. 526 (1969) (equal representation principle regarding congressional district plans applied with severity amounting to a constitutional rule). See also City of New Orleans v. Dukes, 427 U.S. 297, 303 (1976); Village of Belle Terre v. Boraas, 416 U.S. 1, 8 (1974); McLaughlin v. Florida, 379 U.S. 184, 192, 196 and concurring opinion of Stewart, J., 198 (1964); Day-Brite Lighting, Inc. v. Missouri, 342 U.S. 421, 423 (1952).

76. E.g., People ex rel. Orcutt v. Instantship Denver, Inc., 176 Colo. 396, 490 P.2d 941 (1971); Pierce v. Incorporated Town of LaPorte City, 259 Iowa 1120, 146 N.W.2d 907 (1966); City of Crowley Firemen v. City of Crowley, 280 So.2d 897 (La. 1973); Maryland State Board of Barber Examiners v. Kuhn, 270 Md. 496, 312 A.2d 216 (1973); In re Martin, 88 Nev. 666, 504 P.2d 14 (1972); Hartford Accident and Indemnity Co. v. Ingram, 290 N.C. 457, 226 S.E.2d 498 (1976); Town of Caledonia v. Racine Limestone Co., Inc., 266 Wis. 475, 63 N.W.2d 697 (1954).

77. Larson v. Lesser, 106 So.2d 188 (Fla. 1958); S. Bloom, Inc. v. Makin, 61 Ill. 2d 70, 329 N.E.2d 213 (1975); Shearer v. Perry Community School District, 236 N.W.2d 688 (Iowa, 1975); Federal Distillers, Inc. v. State, 304

Minn. 28, 229 N.W.2d 144 (1975); Hartford Accident and Indemity Co. v. Ingram, 290 N.C. 457, 226 S.E.2d 498 (1976); State v. Memorial Gardens Development Corporation, 143 W. Va. 182, 101 S.E.2d 425 (1958).

78. Leading cases exemplifying the categories of preferred values are (1) on race: McLaughlin v. Florida, 379 U.S. 184 (1964); (2) on discrimination against interstate commerce: Dean Milk Co. v. City of Madison, 340 U.S. 349 (1951), and Baldwin v. Seelig, 294 U.S. 511 (1935); (3) on burdening public policy-making processes: Kramer v. Union Free School District, 395 U.S. 621 (1969) (right to vote), Swann v. Adams, 385 U.S. 440 (1967) (congressional districts), Schneider v. State, 308 U.S. 147 (1939) (freedom of speech in public affairs); (4) on freedom of expression in the arts: Joseph Burstyn, Inc. v. Wilson, 343 U.S. 495 (1962); and (5) on protection of individual privacy and dignity: Roe v. Wade, 410 U.S. 113 (1973), Griswold v. Connecticut, 381 U.S. 479 (1965), and Skinner v. Oklahoma, 316 U.S. 535 (1942).

79. See notes 5, 25, 26, and 41, *supra.*

80. 379 U.S. 184 (1964).

81. Epperson v. Arkansas, 393 U.S. 97, 103 (1968); Gomillion v. Lightfoot, 364 U.S. 339, 342 (1960); DeJonge v. Oregon, 299 U.S. 353, 362, 365 (1937).

82. Village of Arlington Heights v. Metropolitan Housing Development Corporation, 429 U.S. 252, 265–68 (1977), and Washington v. Davis, 426 U.S. 229, 243, 248 (1976) (disproportionate impact of legislation on blacks not alone enough to establish invalidity, but indication that, after such showing, supporter must show valid public interest served).

83. See Nixon v. Administrator of General Services, 433 U.S. 425, 467–68 (1977); Planned Parenthood of Central Missouri v. Danforth, 428 U.S. 52, 66–67 (1976); Salyer Land Co. v. Tulare Lake Basin Water Storage District, 410 U.S. 719, 728–30 (1973).

84. McLaughlin v. Florida, 379 U.S. 184, 196 (1964).

85. First National Bank of Boston v. Belotti, 435 U.S. 765, 786 (1978); Williams v. Rhodes, 393 U.S. 23, 31 (1968); Bates v. Little Rock, 361 U.S. 516, 524 (1960).

86. The Sinking Fund Cases, 99 U.S. 700, 718 (1879).

87. Smith v. Daily Mail Publishing Co., 443 U.S. 97, 102 (1979) (free press); Hunt v. Washington State Apple Advertising Commission, 432 U.S. 333, 353 (1977) (discrimination against interstate commerce).

88. Central Hudson Gas & Electric Corporation v. Public Service Commission of New York, 100 Sup. Ct. 2343 (1980); Virginia State Board of Pharmacy v. Virginia Citizens Consumer Council, 425 U.S. 748, 770 (1976).

89. Califano v. Westcott, 443 U.S. 76, 89 (1979); Personnel Administrator of Massachusetts v. Feeney, 442 U.S. 256, 273 (majority), 286 (dissent) (1979); Craig v. Boren, 429 U.S. 190, 197 (1977).

90. On race: Loving v. Virginia, 388 U.S. 1, 9–10 (1967); McLaughlin v. Florida, 379 U.S. 184, 192 (1964). On discrimination against interstate commerce: H. P. Hood & Sons Inc. v. DuMond, 336 U.S. 525, 533–34 (1949);

Baldwin v. G. A. F. Seeling, Inc., 294 U.S. 511, 522, 523 (1935); Welton v. Missouri, 91 U.S. 275, 280 (1876).

91. Kramer v. Union Free School District, 395 U.S. 621, 626 (1969); Schneider v. State, 308 U.S. 147, 161 (1939).

92. Abood v. Detroit Board of Education, 431 U.S. 209, 231 (1977); Virginia State Board of Pharmacy v. Virginia Citizens Consumer Council, 425 U.S. 748, 761–65 (1976); Bigelow v. Virginia, 421 U.S. 809, 826 (1975); Pittsburgh Press Co. v. Pittsburgh Commission on Human Relations, 413 U.S. 376, 382, 385 (1973). *Cf.* Bates v. State Bar of Arizona, 433 U.S. 350, 363–65, 380–81 (1977) (because of social and functional differences of commercial speech from political speech, overbreadth doctrine not applicable re commercial speech).

93. See Ely 1980, ch. 6.

94. See Griswold v. Connecticut, 381 U.S. 479, 483, 486 (1965) (focus on "privacy" values in ruling against statute penalizing use of contraceptives by married couples); Skinner v. Oklahoma, 316 U.S. 535, 541 (1942) (along with emphasis on social dangers, stress on peculiar impact on individual of compulsory sterlization law).

95. *Cf.* Lowi 1969:85–97 and Truman 1951;352–94 (power of lobbies). See Ely 1980, ch. 6, for an able argument that strict judicial scrutiny should extend to all situations in which maldistribution of benefits of legal order flows from unequal participation in policymaking processes.

96. See Daniel v. Family Security Life Insurance Co., 336 U.S. 220, 224 (1949). *Cf.* Rehnquist, J., dissenting, in Sugarman v. Dougall, 413 U.S. 634, 656 (1972); ("The mere recitation of the words 'insular and discrete minority' is hardly a *constitutional* reason for prohibiting state legislative classifications. . . . Our society, consisting of over 200 million individuals of multitudinous origins, customs, tongues, beliefs, and cultures is, to say the least, diverse. It would hardly take extraordinary ingenuity for a lawyer to find 'insular and discrete' minorities at every turn in the road. Yet unless the Court can precisely define and constitutionally justify both the terms and analysis it uses, these decisions today stand for the proposition that the Court can choose a 'minority' differently from the 'majority'. I cannot find, and the Court does not cite, any constitutional authority for such a 'ward of the Court' approach to equal protection."

97. See Holmes, "Natural Law," 1920:310, 312; Patterson 1953:332, 362–66.

98. See United States v. Carolene Products Co., 304 U.S. 144, 152–53, n.4 (1938); West Coast Hotel Co. v. Parrish, 300 U.S. 379, 400 (1937), expressly overruling the doctrine declared in Adkins v. Children's Hospital, 261 U.S. 525, 546 (1923).

99. See Hampton v. Mow Sun Wong, 426 U.S. 88, 102–3 (1976); Board of Regents v. Roth, 408 U.S. 564, 577 (1972) and Perry v. Sindermann, 408 U.S. 593, 602–3 (1972). *Cf.* Smith 1977:609–17 (job control as means of political repression).

100. On abortion: Roe v. Wade, 410 U.S. 113, 155–56, 163 (1973). On contraceptives: Eisenstadt v. Baird, 405 U.S. 438, 453 (1972); Griswold v. Connecticut, 381 U.S. 479, 485–86 (1965).

101. Kleppe v. New Mexico, 426 U.S. 529, 536 (1976) ("Property belonging to the United States"); Helvering v. Davis, 301 U.S. 619, 640 (1937) (congressional appropriations).

102. Maher v. Roe, 432 U.S. 464, 479 (1977).

103. Dandridge v. Williams, 397 U.S. 471, 487 (1970).

104. San Antonio Independent School District v. Rodriguez, 411 U.S. 1, 23, 28, 43 (1973).

105. See Marshall, J., dissenting, in Beal v. Doe, 432 U.S. 438, 457, 458 (1977); San Antonio Independent School District v. Rodriguez, 411 U.S. 1, 109 (1973); Dandridge v. Williams, 397 U.S. 471, 522 (1970).

106. This policy comes close to expression in Maher v. Roe, 432 U.S. 464, 471, 479 (1977), and in the dissent of Harlan, J., in Douglas v. California, 372 U.S. 353, 361–62 (1963). For another reflection of the degree of policy discretion exercised in elaborating preferred-value doctrine, see the exchanges in Carey v. Population Services International among the plurality, 431 U.S. 678, 688, n.5, and 693, n.15 (1977), and Powell, J., concurring, *id.*, 705, and Rehnquist, J., dissenting, *id.*, 718. See a somewhat similar exchange between the majority and Rehnquist, J., dissenting (joined by Burger, CJ., Stewart and Blackmun, JJ.), Trimble v. Gordon, 430 U.S. 762, 767, 769, 772, 781, 784 (1977). The federal courts have not been unwilling to enter judgments or decrees that require spending public money to bring matters into compliance with the court's order. E.g., Milliken v. Bradley, 433 U.S. 267 (1977); Griffin v. County School Board, 377 U.S. 218 (1964). However, such decisions seem to derive from the Court's concern that its own judgments be effectual and respected; they do not focus on the legislature's general control of the public purse or point toward such broad judicial scrutiny of the purse power as would be indicated by ruling that any statutory appropriation is "suspect" if the public spending may operate less favorably to individuals of small means than to those of more wealth or income.

SOURCES CITED

[Official action documents are cited in full in Notes.]

Anderson, Frederick R. *NEPA in the Courts: Legal Analysis of the National Environmental Protection Act*. Baltimore: Johns Hopkins University Press, 1973.

Berger, Raoul. *Government by Judiciary*. Cambridge, Mass.: Harvard University Press, 1977.

Beuscher, Jacob H. "The Use of Experts by Courts." 54 *Harvard Law Review* 1105 (1941).

Bickel, Alexander and Harry H. Wellington. "Legislative Purpose and the Judicial Process: The Lincoln Mills Case." 71 *Harvard Law Review* 1 (1957).

Bogart, Ernest L. *Economic History of the American People*. 2d ed. New York: Longmans, Green, 1938.

Bolling, Richard. *House Out of Order* New York: E.P. Dutton, 1966.

Broude, Henry W. "The Role of the State in American Economic Development, 1820–1890." In Hugh G. J. Aitken, ed., *The State and Economic Growth*. New York: Social Science Research Council, 1959.

Bunn, George and Jeff Gallagher. "Legislative Committee Review of Administrative Rules in Wisconsin." 1977 *Wisconsin Law Review* 935.

Calhoun, John C. *A Disquisition on Government*. Richard Cralle, ed. New York: Peter Smith, 1943; original, 1853.

Carosso, Vincent P. *Investment Banking in America*. Cambridge, Mass.: Harvard University Press, 1970.

Cary, William L. *Politics and the Regulatory Agencies.* Ann Arbor: University of Michigan Press, 1967.

Chamberlain, Joseph P. *Legislative Processes, National and State.* New York: D. Appleton-Century, 1936.

Chamberlain, Lawrence H. *The President, Congress, and Legislation.* New York: Columbia University Press, 1947.

Chicago, University of. Staff of Social Sciences I. *The People Shall Judge,* 2 vols. Chicago: University of Chicago, 1949.

Clapp, Charles L. *The Congressman: His Work As He Sees It.* Washington, D.C.: Brookings Institution, 1963.

Cohen, Julius. "Hearings on a Bill: Legislative Folklore?" 37 *Minnesota Law Review* 34 (1952).

Committee on American Legislatures, American Political Science Association. *Report on American State Legislatures.* New York: Thomas Y. Crowell, 1954.

Congressional Research Service, Library of Congress, *The Constitution of the United States of America: An Analysis and Interpretation.* Washington, D.C.: Government Printing Office, 1973.

Corwin, Edward S. *The President: Office and Powers, 1787–1957.* 4th rev. ed. New York: New York University Press, 1957.

Dahl, Robert A. and Charles E. Lindblom. *Politics, Economics, and Welfare.* New York: Harper & Brothers, 1953.

Davis, Kenneth C. *Discretionary Justice.* Baton Rouge: Louisiana State University Press, 1969.

Derthick, Martha. *Policymaking for Social Security.* Washington, D.C.: The Brookings Institution, 1979.

Dickerson, Reed. *The Interpretation and Application of Statutes.* Boston: Little, Brown, 1975.

Dodd, Lawrence C. and Richard L. Schott. *Congress and the Administrative State.* New York: Wiley, 1979.

Duffy, James. *Domestic Affairs: American Programs and Priorities.* New York: Simon & Schuster, 1978.

Ely, John Hart. *Democracy and Distrust: A Theory of Judicial Review.* Cambridge, Mass.: Harvard University Press, 1980.

Federalist, The Henry Cabot Lodge, ed. New York: Putnam, 1907.

Fenno, Richard R., Jr. *The Power of the Purse: Appropriations Politics In Congress.* Boston: Little, Brown, 1966.

Freund, Ernst. *Standards of American Legislation.* Chicago: University of Chicago Press, 1917.

Friedman, Lawrence M. *A History of American Law*. New York: Simon and Schuster, 1973.

Gray, John Chipman. *The Nature and Sources of the Law*. New York: Columbia University Press, 1909.

Gross, Bertram. *The Legislative Struggle*. New York: McGraw-Hill, 1953.

Gunn, L. Ray. "The New York State Legislature: A Developmental Perspective, 1777–1846." *Social Science History* (1980), 4: 267.

Hand, Learned. *The Spirit of Liberty: Papers and Addresses*, Irving Dilliard, ed. New York: Vintage Books, 1959.

Handlin, Oscar and Mary F. Handlin. *Commonwealth: A Study of the Role of Government in the American Economy: Massachusetts, 1774–1861*. New York: New York University Press, 1947.

Hartz, Louis. *Economic Policy and Democratic Thought: Pennsylvania, 1776–1860*. Cambridge, Mass.: Harvard University Press, 1948.

Heath, Milton S. *Constructive Liberalism: The Role of the State in Economic Development in Georgia to 1860*. Cambridge, Mass.: Harvard University Press, 1954.

Heller, Walter W. *New Dimensions of Political Economy*. Cambridge, Mass.: Harvard University Press, 1966.

Hibbard, Benjamin H. *A History of the Public Lands Policies*. Madison: University of Wisconsin Press, 1965.

Hockett, Homer Carey. *The Constitutional History of the United States*. 2 vols. New York: Macmillan, 1939.

Holmes, O. W., Jr. *The Common Law* Boston: Little, Brown, 1881.

——Collected Legal Papers. New York: Harcourt, Brace, 1921.

Hurst, James Willard. *The Growth of American Law: The Law Makers* Boston: Little, Brown, 1950.

——*Law and Economic Growth: The Legal History of the Lumber Industry in Wisconsin, 1836–1915*. Cambridge, Mass.: Harvard University Press, 1964.

——*The Legitimacy of the Business Corporation in the Law of the United States, 1780–1970*. Charlottesville: University Press of Virginia, 1970.

——*A Legal History of Money in the United States*. Lincoln: University of Nebraska Press, 1973.

——"Watergate: Some Basic Issues." *Center Magazine* (1974), 7:11.

——*Law and Social Order in the United States*. Ithaca, N.Y.: Cornell University Press, 1977.

——"Alexander Hamilton, Law Maker." 78 *Columbia Law Review* 483 (1978).

Jackson, Robert H. "The Meaning of Statutes." 34 *American Bar Association Journal* 535 (1948).

Jaffe, Louis. *Judicial Control of Administrative Action*. Boston: Little, Brown, 1965.

Jones, Harry W. "Statutory Doubts and Legislative Intention." 40 *Columbia Law Review* 957 (1940).

Koenig, Louis W. *The Chief Executive*. New York: Harcourt, Brace & World, 1964.

Landis, James. M. "Constitutional Limitations on the Congressional Power of Investigation." 40 *Harvard Law Review* 153 (1926).

——"Note on Statutory Interpretation." 43 *Harvard Law Review* 886 (1930).

——*The Administrative Process*. New Haven, Conn.: Yale University Press, 1938.

Lekachman, Robert. *The Age of Keynes*. New York: Random House, 1966.

Letwin, William. *Law and Economic Policy in America*. New York: Random House, 1965.

Levy, Leonard W. *The Law of the Commonwealth and Chief Justice Shaw*. New York: Harper Torchbooks, 1967.

Lindblom, Charles. *Politics and Markets*. New York: Basic Books, 1977.

Linde, Hans and George Bunn. *Legislative and Administrative Processes*. Mineola, N.Y.: Foundation Press, 1976.

Llewellyn, Karl N. *The Common Law Tradition: Deciding Appeals*. Boston: Little, Brown, 1960.

Locke, John. *The Second Treatise of Civil Government*. J.W. Gough, ed. Oxford: Basil Blackwell, 1946.

Lowi, Theodore J. *The End of Liberalism*. New York: Norton, 1969.

Lynd, Robert S. and Helen Merrell Lynd. *Middletown*. New York: Harcourt, Brace, 1929.

Macaulay, Stewart. "Lawyers and Consumer Protection Laws." 14 *Law and Society Review* 115 (1979).

McCloskey, Robert G. *The American Supreme Court*. Chicago: University of Chicago Press, 1960.

Mayhew, David R. *Congress: The Electoral Connection*. New Haven, Conn.: Yale University Press, 1974.

Mermin, Samuel. *Law and the Legal System.* Boston: Little, Brown, 1973.

Miller, Merle. *Lyndon.* New York: Putnam, 1980.

Neustadt, Richard E. *Presidential Power.* New York: New American Library, Signet, 1964.

Patterson, Edwin W. *Jurisprudence: Men and Ideas of the Law.* Brooklyn: Foundation Press, 1953.

Potts, C.S. "Power of Legislative Bodies to Punish for Contempts." 74 *University of Pennsylvania Law Review* 691, 780 (1926).

Prosser, William. *Law of Torts.* 4th ed. St. Paul, Minn.: West, 1971.

Radin, Max. *On Anglo-American Legal History.* St. Paul, Minn.: West, 1936.

——"Statutory Interpretation." 43 *Harvard Law Review* 863 (1930).

——"A Short Way with Statutes." 56 *Harvard Law Review* 388 (1942).

Redman, Eric. *The Dance of Legislation.* New York: Simon & Schuster, 1973.

Richardson, James D., ed. *A Compilation of Messages and Papers of the Presidents, 1789–1897.* 10 vols. Washington, D.C.: Government Printing Office, 1896.

Scheiber, Harry N. *Ohio Canal Era: A Case Study of Government and the Economy, 1820–1861.* Athens: Ohio University Press, 1969.

Smith, Hedrick. *The Russians.* New York: Ballantine Books, 1977.

Smithies, Arthur. *The Budgetary Process in the United States.* New York: McGraw-Hill, 1955.

Stewart, Richard. "The Reformation of American Administrative Law." 88 *Harvard Law Review* 1667 (1975).

Thorelli, Hans B. *The Federal Antitrust Policy.* Baltimore: Johns Hopkins University Press, 1955.

Thurow, Lester C. *The Zero-Sum Society.* New York: Basic Books, 1980.

Tocqueville, Alexis de. *Democracy in America.* Phillips Bradley, ed. 2 vols. New York: Knopf, 1951.

Tribe, Laurence H. *American Constitutional Law.* Mineola, N.Y.: Foundation Press, 1978.

Truman, David B. *The Governmental Process.* New York: Knopf, 1951.

Walker, Harvey. *Law Making in the United States.* New York: Ronald Press, 1934.

White, Leonard D. *The Republican Era: 1869–1901, A Study in Administrative History.* New York: Macmillan, 1958.

Witte, Edwin E. *The Development of the Social Security Act*. Madison: University of Wisconsin Press, 1962.

Wooddy, Carroll H. "The Growth of Governmental Functions." In *Report of the President's Research Committee on Social Trends, Recent Social Trends in the United States*. New York: Whittlesey House, McGraw-Hill, 1934.

INDEX